Y0-CCV-257

ALCOHOLISM IN THE PROFESSIONS

ALCOHOLISM
IN THE PROFESSIONS

LeClair Bissell, M.D.
Paul W. Haberman

New York   Oxford
OXFORD UNIVERSITY PRESS
1984

Copyright © 1984 by Oxford University Press, Inc.

Library of Congress Cataloging in Publication Data

Bissell, LeClair.
  Alcoholism in the professions.

  Includes bibliographical references and index.
    1. Alcoholism—United States. 2. Professional
employees—United States—Alcohol use. 3. Alcoholism—
Treatment—United States. I. Haberman, Paul W.,
1928-   . II. Title.
HV5142.B57 1984   362.2′92′0880622   84-815
ISBN 0-19-503459-7

Printed in the United States of America
Printing (last digit): 9 8 7 6 5 4 3 2 1

Preface

Alcoholism is the most common, serious illness likely to affect a professional in the first fifteen years after completing graduate education. While we hear warnings about the potential danger to ourselves from other mood-altering drugs, particularly the illegal ones like cocaine and narcotics, our use of alcohol is rarely discussed. When it is, the topic is usually accompanied by a joke or two and a variety of signals to ensure that the speaker won't be perceived as prudish or not part of the crowd.

I graduated with the class of 1963 from Columbia University's College of Physicians & Surgeons. Although some of us were to enter areas of medicine where nearly half of our future patients would suffer from alcoholism, only five minutes were devoted to this disease in our entire four years of medical school. We were woefully unprepared to deal with it in others, much less to recognize it in ourselves and our colleagues. The vast majority of professional training programs in medicine, law, dentistry, nursing, social work, and the like have not and still do not even now routinely prepare their students any better. Improvement has been fairly recent and is still sporadic. It came too late to reach any but a handful of those who graduated before the mid-1970s.

Medical and nursing school faculty often assert, with complete sincerity, that the charge that alcoholism isn't taught is inaccurate.

They point out that a great deal *is* indeed taught in pathology and other courses about the toxic effects of the drug alcohol on the body. They provide detailed information in pharmacology and physiology courses about alcohol's physiological effects, encompassing everything from the release of antidiuretic hormone to identifying accurately alcohol's role as the most frequent cause of "essential" hypertension. Some schools also do a good job of describing physical dependency on alcohol, the management of delirium tremens, and other alcohol withdrawal states.

Knowing about the physiological and toxic effects of alcohol has little to do with understanding alcoholism. It does not teach us to distinguish an alcoholic from a problem drinker any more than familiarity with the normal metabolism of glucose would be adequate preparation for understanding diabetes. It does not tell us what to say to a patient or how to confront a colleague in trouble. It does not prepare us to understand what is happening if we ourselves or members of our families begin to show tell-tale symptoms. We most certainly are not made aware that denial is the hallmark of this "cunning, baffling and powerful" illness, and so we have floundered. Many of us still are floundering, but there is improvement and hope for change.

The experiences and research that led to this book grew in part from my own history of alcoholism. I stopped drinking altogether in 1953, some years before starting medical school. Since people tend to be particularly interested in those illnesses that have affected them or their families personally and to pay extra attention to what is being taught about them, I was appalled to find only a small part of a single lecture devoted to the disease that had so nearly ended my life. Moreover, I was particularly dismayed by the assertions that all alcoholics suffered from character disorders, commonly exhibited passive-dependent personalities, and found Alcoholics Anonymous (A.A.) useful only as a surrogate family for their dependency needs. The lecturer went on to imply that only nonintellectuals and those able to accept a bible-thumping brand of religious evangelism could find A.A. acceptable. By inference that meant that physicians like ourselves most certainly would not, nor would many of our patients. (Actually the first three A.A. members were a stockbroker, a surgeon, and an attorney in that order. Moreover, A.A. is careful not to espouse any particular religious orientation, to accommodate with ease a variety of Christians and Jews, among others.)

These inaccuracies continued to bother me. I rather expected that more and better information would follow during the clinical years, but it didn't. Except for an occasional anecdote, usually written as an anonymous first-person case history, I found the medical literature devoid of the experience of professionals who had recovered. At that time there was almost nothing available on alcoholism in health care or any other profession.

I decided someday to attempt face-to-face interviews with perhaps 100 A.A. members who were physicians and report the results. The very existence of the sample would demonstrate that physicians not only do develop alcoholism but also that they can find A.A. acceptable. As I asked questions and sought to locate the physicians to be interviewed, friends and colleagues increasingly shared anecdotes and newspaper clippings, described their concern about some of our alcoholic peers, and suggested that we include in the study certain other professional groups as well.

Some of what we learned in the initial interview has been published elsewhere, but these papers were subject to the limitations of appearing singly and scattered among several different journals. This book permits a comparison of the experiences in five different professions as well as a description of what happened over a period of five to seven years to the 407 people we initially interviewed.

It lets us report on what happened to these men and women not only during the course of their drinking, but for several years of their recovery. In addition, it describes the response of the professions then and now and indicates the present policies and formal response of the major national organizations to alcoholism in their memberships. It catalogs many of the support and intervention groups currently available specifically for alcoholic professionals and their concerned friends and family. We have tried to make clear which services are confidential and which are not. Whenever possible, contacts given are those known to be discrete as well as those unlikely soon to be replaced (Appendix C). For this last reason, many individuals named are not the current group officers, but those in the organizations whose addresses will remain as listed for some time.

I hope that much of what follows will soon be out of date and even regarded as primitive. I am not optimistic that this will be the case. While there has been enormous progress in the 20 years since I completed medical school, most of our alcoholic colleagues in most of the major professions are still left to their own devices and many still die of its complications while their alcoholism itself goes unacknowledged and untreated.

                                                            LeC. B.

Acknowledgments

Many people helped with this project since it began in the late 1960s. Margaret Bailey and Barry Leach lent portions of their original questionnaire; Paul W. Haberman, coauthor of this book, assisted in the preparation of the monograph based on their study. Robert W. Jones was coinvestigator in the early years and worked with us until just before his death. We miss him. Paul picked up when Bob could no longer continue. Jeffrey W. House, Rochelle M. Reinhardt, and Joan Knizeski at Oxford University Press provided us with encouragement and constructive suggestions.

Interviewers, who pursued our subjects for follow-up over much of the United States and Canada and, in one case, all the way to Ireland, cannot as A.A. members be named in full—but Karen G., Leah G., Shirley P., Jo Ann F., Alicia S., and Nancy P. continue to have our appreciation and admiration. We hope we never have to try to hide from them! Denise Hinzpeter capably supervised coders and prepared the initial computer programs. Experienced coders were recruited from students and staff at the Division of Sociomedical Sciences, Columbia University School of Public Health. Jeffrey A. Starr and Teddy Zeitlin at CRC Information Systems, Inc., produced the necessary programming and computer output. Jean Meyer, Beth Kahn, Judy Stires, Joan Cottingham, and Cynthia Clifford wrote the letters, made phone calls, managed the paperwork, and handled the details that no one loves and research requires.

Special thanks to the interview subjects and their families who put up with interviews at inconvenient times and places, met airplanes, created space in busy schedules, offered encouragement and hospitality, and even sent an occasional check to keep the study going when other support seemed likely to fail.

The Smithers Alcoholism Treatment and Training Center of St. Luke's-Roosevelt Hospital made this project possible by giving us and other Smithers staff time to do most of the work on the first interviews in 1968 through 1969; the Center itself exists only through the generosity of Mr. R. Brinkley Smithers himself. (Although Smithers Center has treated and does treat a great many alcoholic professionals, none of the subjects in this study were patients of our own or of the Smithers Center.)

Our sincere thank you for the encouragement and financial support received from the Educational Foundation of America, the Gail and Robert Spiegal Foundation, Donald and Ann Millar, Edgehill Newport, Inc., and the American Medical Association Education and Research Foundation. Staff of the Medical and Health Research Association of New York City, Inc., ably administered the project finances.

We are deeply grateful to Marty M. and to the many men and women of Alcoholics Anonymous who cooperated with us so graciously in our efforts to locate and interview the special and often elusive group within a group, the professionals we are about to describe. Since A.A. keeps essentially no membership lists, is remarkably disinterested in last names, and stubbornly stresses "principles, not personalities," our mutual task was not simple. Bill W., cofounder of A.A., knew and encouraged us. Without his advice and blessing this work could probably not have been done; we could not have followed our research plan while simultaneously observing A.A. traditions. Bill was fond of what he described as a very ancient Middle Eastern greeting, one which well expresses our feeling toward him and so many others of his fellowship who did so much with no expectation of acknowledgment or reward, and again most particularly toward the recovered professionals themselves who shared with remarkable candor their pain and triumph, their experience, strength, and hope—"We salute you and thank you for your lives."

LeC. B.
P. W. H.

Contents

ALCOHOLISM IN THE PROFESSIONS

1

Highlights

The Study

PREVALENCE AND PROCEDURES

Specific information about alcoholism in the professions is still relatively scarce. The first data comparing a substantial number of alcoholics in high-status occupations—medicine, law, dentistry, nursing, and social work—are presented in this book. There are as yet no accurate estimates on the prevalence of alcoholism among the members of specific professional groups, but assuming that professionals are at the same risk as other American adults who drink, roughly one in ten males and one in twenty females will be alcoholic or experience a serious drinking problem. Rates thus should be higher in professions like medicine, law, and dentistry, where men predominate, than in nursing or social work. Despite a narrowing gender gap in both career choice and alcoholism, there are still more alcoholic men than women.

There is also little information on treatment outcome for alcoholics in the professions. In addition to methodological problems common to most treatment evaluation, rarely is there any attempt to compare professional groups of patients with each other or with other patients in the same treatment setting. Prevalence estimates of alcoholism in the professions tend to be of questionable validity and deal primarily with physicians and nurses.

It is commonly claimed that alcoholism is unusually prevalent among physicians and nurses because a disproportionately large percentage of them are found among psychiatric inpatients or outpatients. Physicians have also been shown to have a disproportionately high mortality rate from cirrhosis of the liver, which may, however, be the result of hepatitis rather than alcoholism. Another explanation, suggested by our study findings, for the relatively large number of alcoholic doctors and nurses in treatment is that these professionals were treated as hospital inpatients and sought help from psychiatrists much more often than those in the other professional groups.

Each of our subjects on average was aware of four others in the same profession currently in trouble with alcohol. If 9 percent of male drinkers and 5 percent of female drinkers are at substantial risk of developing alcoholism or a serious drinking problem, and if only 70 percent of our professionals drink and half of the 2.2 million drinkers in these professions are women, then these groups alone should contain more than 150,000 who are or will be in trouble with alcohol.

During the study years, we estimated that, of 108,000 dentists, 8 percent, or 9,000, were alcoholic. Since it is believed that only 10 percent of alcoholics find their way into A.A. or treatment, there should have been only about 900 dentists who received or were receiving help. Thus, the 49 dentists we readily located for interviewing would have comprised more than 5 percent of all the available recovered dentists in A.A. After an exhaustive literature review, we cannot at present say with any certainty how many members of any profession already are or will become alcoholic.

As treaters of others, professionals may be unusually slow to seek help for alcoholism. Inappropriate treatment and long delays in intervention have been the rule. We cannot know how much harm is actually done to patients or clients by the alcoholic or drug-using professional, but it must be significant. Generally, professional intervention still takes place quite late in a drinking career and usually even then only when some other agency has first become involved.

Many alcoholics attempt to decrease their drinking by using other mood-changing drugs, usually sedatives and tranquilizers.

In the medical professions, alcoholics are not as limited in their choice of drugs because of availability and can obtain a variety of agents, including narcotics, without becoming involved in the illicit drug culture. In our study, the difference between medical and nonmedical professional groups reporting addiction to a drug in addition to alcohol was not very substantial—39 percent and 32 percent, respectively. However, physicians and nurses reported an addiction to narcotics more often than did lawyers and college women.

All 407 subjects interviewed for this study described themselves as alcoholics and A.A. members who had reportedly done no drinking whatsoever for the past year. Reinterviews were conducted five to seven years after the first interview, with a follow-up rate of almost 90 percent.

The total sample consisted of 214 men and 193 women. The 97 physicians and 49 dentists were all male; the 100 nurses and 56 college women were all female; and 49 of 55 attorneys and 19 of 50 social workers were men. The physicians, dentists, registered nurses, and attorneys had all received the degrees required to practice their professions; the social workers all had earned M.S.W. degrees, and the college women had completed at least three years of college, with 61 percent earning at least a bachelor's degree. Overall, reinterviews were obtained for 362 subjects, including 12 with next of kin when the subject was deceased. By profession, follow-up rates ranged from 84 percent to 95 percent, with very little sex-related differences.

The median ages of men and women in our study were 51 and 46, respectively. Most of the subjects were white and born in the United States. About one-fifth of both men and women were Phi Beta Kappa or had received honors in college, and more than three-fifths of each reported graduating in the top third of their professional school class. Men reported more years of sobriety than did the women, probably reflecting their age differences.

The topics in the first interview included the subjects' background, their drinking history, eight benchmarks or important drinking milestones associated with alcoholism, use of and addiction to other mood-altering drugs, experiences related to drinking and alcoholism, overdoses and suicide attempts, professional or legal sanctions related to drinking, treatment and A.A. experiences, familial alcoholism, and alcohol-related attitudes or opinions. Topics in the reinterview included sobriety or relapses, other drug use, and related problems or changes experienced between the interviews. (Abridged items included in the two questionnaires are presented in Appendix A.)

Respondents were first classified according to whether or not they had in the first interview reported ever having been addicted either to nonnarcotic mood-altering drugs or to narcotics. Almost all of those reporting addiction to narcotics reported that they had also been addicted to nonnarcotics. Subjects were then classified into three "addiction groups": alcohol alone; alcohol plus non-narcotics, including 12 addicted to "soft" narcotics, for example, codeine, but not to "hard" drugs; and alcohol plus narcotics, that is, with an addiction to drugs such as morphine.

COURSE OF ALCOHOL AND OTHER DRUG USE

Regardless of their profession or addiction to other drugs, for men and women the benchmarks for sequence and age of onset of initial drinking were very similar. Respondents tended to get drunk for the first time in their late teens. Two years later they began to drink on a regular basis at a median age of 19 for men and 21 for women. If this seems relatively late, it should be noted that 45 percent of the respondents were 50 years of age or older when first interviewed and about one-quarter grew up before prohibition was repealed. Getting drunk with some regularity began at a median age of 26 regardless of sex.

It is very difficult to pinpoint the exact onset of a disease that typically is slowly progressive, episodic, shows marked diversity in the related signs or symptoms, and in addition carries a high degree of social stigma. Nevertheless, several drinking benchmarks in our study are useful in identifying the onset of active alcoholism: when a person begins to get drunk with some regularity, when drinking first begins to interfere with his or her life, when someone else first expresses concern about the subject's drinking, and when personal concern begins. The typical course we observed almost without exception was getting drunk with some regularity, with drinking first beginning to interfere with the respondent's life about three years later. Someone else first expressed concern two years after that point and, within the next year, the respondent first became concerned about his or her own drinking.

The criterion we prefer for the onset of alcoholism is when drinking first begins to interfere with the person's life. Five of the six groups in our study obtained their professional degrees or completed their basic professional training at least four years on average before the onset of alcoholism as we have defined it. The social workers are atypical because 44 percent obtained their master's degree after they had recovered from alcoholism.

Respondents attended their first A.A. meeting at a median age of 40, about 11 years after drinking started to interfere, and they had their last drink two years later at a median age of 42. The drinking history among women in our study showed interference 7 years after beginning to drink regularly, compared to 11 years for the men. This "telescoping effect," a term used to describe the more rapid progression said to be common in women, also was observed for addiction to other drugs, but did not seem as large. Women also demonstrated a shorter period of active alcoholism (considered the interval from the time when drinking first interfered to the last drink) than did the men.

Approximately two-fifths of both the men and women had received psychiatric treatment for their alcoholism before achieving sobriety in A.A. Sixty-eight percent of the men and 58 percent of the women had been institutionalized at least once for alcoholism, with their first admissions occurring at the median ages of 39 years and 34 years, respectively. The men first became concerned about their own drinking when slightly older than the women, although there was no gender difference in their ages when another person expressed concern.

Overall, 33 of the subjects reported previous, self-defined "addiction" to "hard" narcotics in the first interview; 14 and 12 percent of physicians and nurses did. The 197 respondents in these two professions, comprising 48 percent of the sample, thus accounted for 79 percent of the professionals reporting "hard" narcotic addiction.

While access influenced the category of drugs complicating alcoholism, secondary addictions per se were unexpectedly almost as common for men and women both overall and according to drug category. Thirty-six percent of all subjects reported being addicted to drugs other than alcohol before the first interview, ranging from 27 percent of the largely male attorneys to 43 percent of the all-male group of physicians. One-quarter of all subjects reported being addicted to nonnarcotic drugs only. Of those who reported being addicted to "hard" or "soft" narcotics, 87 percent had been addicted to other mood-altering drugs as well.

Looking at use alone rather than "addiction," 84 percent of all subjects—91 percent of the women and 79 percent of the men—reported having used a variety of mood-altering drugs. One-fifth of the medical professionals and men compared to 11 percent of the nonmedical professionals and 14 percent of the women were at least occasionally using some mood-changing drug at the time of the initial interview. Use of mood-altering drugs did not inevitably lead to addiction to them, but if one looks at only those who say they were exposed, the overall percent addicted to other drugs, of course, increases and men then actually report "addiction" somewhat more often than women. The percentages of all *users*, male users, and female users addicted to other drugs are 43, 48, and 39 percent, respectively.

Of the total sample, barbiturates and amphetamines had been most commonly used, by 48 percent and 44 percent, respectively, followed by minor tranquilizers and codeine. About 10 percent more women than men reported using amphetamines, other mood elevators, meprobamate, and phenothiazines.

Follow-up respondents were asked about the order in which they first had used alcohol and other drugs. Nine-tenths reported that alcohol was the first mood-altering substance they had used, including 12 percent who had never used any other drug, followed in order by nonnarcotics and then by "hard" narcotics or codeine. Of the 320 previous smokers who were followed up, 41 percent had stopped. Surprisingly, medical professionals were less likely to have stopped smoking than others.

Of the entire sample, 35 percent had at least one alcoholic parent, including 41 percent of the women, compared to 29 percent of the men. A total of 120 subjects had alcoholic fathers, 48 had alcoholic mothers, and 26 reported that both parents were alcoholic. The median age at which men *without* alcoholic fathers started drinking regularly was 19; the sons of alcoholic fathers delayed slightly to a median age of 20. The women with an alcoholic father started to drink regularly at age 19, whereas the women in the sample without an alcoholic parent did not start drinking until age 21.

Alcoholic siblings were reported by 29 percent of the men and 31 percent of the women. At initial interview, 10 percent of the men and 6 percent of the women reported having a child who was alcoholic; at follow-up, these proportions were 12 percent and 14 percent, respectively. Moreover, at follow-up, 18 of the 47 subjects with alcoholic children reported that at least one was already in A.A.

CONSEQUENCES AND SANCTIONS

Overt suicide attempts before the first interview were reported by 17 percent of the men and 30 percent of the women. Of those who had attempted suicide, 55 percent had made a single attempt and 73 percent said that their first attempt had occurred before the age of 40. There was a strong correlation between the use of other drugs and a history of attempted suicide; attempts were reported by 16 percent reporting a history of addiction to alcohol alone, by 30 percent addicted to nonnarcotics or codeine, and by 52 percent of the 33 subjects with a history of "hard" narcotic addiction. Of the reinterviewed attempters, 57 percent had taken drug overdoses, most were under the influence of alcohol, and virtually all were under the influence of some drug. (We had not asked for details about these attempts at first interview.)

Less than half of the subjects reported experiencing professional and legal sanctions because of drinking—for example, admonishments from colleagues, warnings from an employer or professional society, loss of driver's license, and arrest or imprisonment. These sanctions were all experienced much more frequently by men than women. Most often sanctioned were those alcoholics also addicted to narcotics and, least often, those not addicted to any other drugs.

Medical professionals reported 4.8 alcohol-related hospital admissions compared to 2.3 for the nonmedical groups. Physicians had the most admissions—an average of 6.3 separate hospitalizations and 4.7 months in hospitals—followed by nurses. Attorneys on average had the fewest admissions (1.9) and spent the least time as inpatients (less than four weeks). All subjects combined had a total of over 1,500 alcohol-related admissions!

Throughout their entire drinking careers, more than three-quarters of the nurses, more than two-fifths of the physicians, and about two-thirds of those in the other professions could not remember any colleague or superior ever saying anything critical to them about their drinking. Yet 62 percent reported drinking during working hours, ranging from 37 percent of the nurses to 80 percent of the attorneys. Furthermore, 60 percent of the sample reported regular morning drinking and 76 percent acknowledged drinking to relieve withdrawal symptoms.

Just over one-quarter of men and women alike had experienced periods of unemployment other than when institutionalized that they attributed directly to drinking. The women had attained and ended their most prestigious jobs before they stopped drinking at median ages of 29 and 34 compared to median ages of 32 and 44 for the men. These differences are probably indicative of the differences in the number of years of professional training, child-care responsibilities, and investment in job stability. Median annual earnings for the men were more than three times greater than for women, reflecting differences between the better paying, predominantly male professions we studied and the poorer paying, predominantly female professions.

Nearly one-quarter of the physicians had been confronted by an employer or medical society and had lost hospital privileges. For varying reasons, equivalent sanctions occurred less frequently in the other professions. As expected, formal sanctions were most often applied to the "hard" narcotic addicts, although they reported no greater number of informal sanctions than did the others. Even simple, informal admonishment was absent for three-quarters of the women and half of the men. An entire drinking career thus ran its course for more than two-thirds of the total sample without a single direct comment about drinking from any colleague or superior that could be remembered!

Only seven physicians and three nurses had lost their licenses to practice, and all but two nurses had regained them. Seven physicians and four dentists had been sued for malpractice, but not necessarily for alcohol-related actions. Almost all entered treatment with license intact and practice having continued up to, or close to, the time of admission.

Despite the relative absence of professional response to the distress of alcoholic colleagues, most of our respondents reported signs of advanced alcoholism. About nine-tenths of both male and female respondents reported such alcoholism-related experiences as loss of control and blackouts. Between 58 and 76 percent reported drinking for relief of insomnia, periods of total abstinence, and binges or benders. Smaller proportions reported having experienced auditory or visual hallucinations. Seizures, fatty liver, and gastrointestinal bleeding had occurred in almost one-fifth of the cases, and 7 percent reported cirrhosis of the liver or pancreatitis. Except for using alcohol for insomnia, men reported these symptoms with more or the same frequency as did women.

In general, the alcoholics also addicted to "hard" narcotics were the most likely to report these experiences, followed in order by those addicted to nonnarcotics or codeine, and then by those without any other addictions. Experiences commonly related to physical dependency, such as drinking for relief of withdrawal symptoms like insomnia, regular morning drinking, or seizures, were among those most highly correlated with other drug addictions. Seizures, auditory and visual hallucinations, and liver cirrhosis in particular were markedly associated with "hard" narcotic addiction. Narcotics may have caused some seizures, while others were probably the result of sedative withdrawal.

SEEKING TREATMENT

When an alcoholic seeks help from the clergy, drinking is often mentioned, but rarely as primary. Thirty-five percent of our medical professionals, the only ones asked for this information, had been to clergy for help. In contrast, to approach A.A. signals that one either acknowledges being alcoholic or is at least willing to consider the possibility. Only 11 percent of the medical professionals, one social worker, and no attorneys had initially heard of A.A. as part of their professional training. Many who had heard of it were poorly informed or even misinformed.

Twenty-two percent of the subjects said they had expected A.A.'s religious emphasis to "turn them off," and 12 percent did find that this caused a problem. Forty-one percent did not expect this aspect to cause difficulty, and 37 percent reported not having any expectations whatsoever about religion in A.A. Over one-third said they had had no expectations concerning the socio-economic status of A.A. members; 41 percent found the members to be of higher status than anticipated, while 20 percent found them to be lower. Only 3 percent found about what they had expected.

At first interview, there was wide variation in the number of meetings that subjects had attended. Nonetheless, 97 percent said that they had attended A.A. meetings one or more times in the previous year; three-fifths attended meetings at least once a week; and 5 percent of these went daily. Those who were more newly sober went more frequently than those who had been abstinent longer.

Forty-three percent of our subjects had seen one or more psychiatrists before A.A. sobriety. Other than clergy and physicians, relatively few professionals were consulted for help; only 13 percent of our subjects ever went to psychologists or social workers. Twenty-three percent of the men, including 39 percent of the physicians, and one-tenth of the women reported that a person treating them specifically denied that they were alcoholic. Furthermore, 40 percent of the men and 19 percent of the women in those groups who said they had told the whole truth about their drinking to a treating person had still had their alcoholism specifically denied.

Relatively few subjects reported being sent by professionals to A.A. or to a specialized alcoholism treatment facility. Systems for identifying the "impaired professional" were virtually nonexistent. Other addictive drugs were frequently and naively offered as substitutes for alcohol. Patients were urged to control rather than to stop drinking, and denial of alcoholism as the primary illness was commonplace. Events that contained clues of alcoholism and could have been used for diagnosis and referral for more definitive treatment were rarely followed up. Our subjects offered innumerable anecdotes of an almost global refusal on the part of all concerned to acknowledge and address their drinking problem.

About one-half of the men and women reported at the initial interview that their first A.A. meeting and last drink occurred at the same time. One-fifth of both sexes reported no further drinking after their first year in A.A. For the others, there were a series of exploratory visits and sometimes even lengthy attendance punctuated with many relapses before a satisfactory alliance was made and the drinking ended.

Thirty-eight percent of the men and 22 percent of the women cited family pressure as the event precipitating their A.A. contact. Health problems were cited by 28 percent of the women and 23 percent of the men. Economic pressure and professional difficulties were mentioned by 17 percent of the men and 9 percent of the women.

Almost all the subjects thought that an alcoholic could not return safely to drinking, although a handful replied "very rarely."

When asked "If you *could* drink safely, would you?" only 26 percent said that, yes, they would. Many volunteered that they felt relieved rather than deprived by the absence of alcohol in their lives. Others made it very clear that "social drinking" did not appeal to them because they were interested in drinking primarily to feel the drug effect. Fewer women than men believed an alcoholic could return safely to normal drinking; but 36 percent of the women, compared to 18 percent of the men, indicated that they would like to drink if it were safe.

Twenty-eight percent of the medical professionals, the only group asked about psychiatric care after drinking had ceased, reported that they were still in this treatment when first interviewed. A.A. and other help were seen as complementary by these subjects, but they agreed that complete withdrawal from alcohol and other drugs had to be addressed first.

SOBRIETY AND RELAPSES

All of the 362 subjects whom we interviewed a second time in person or for whom we interviewed a close relative face-to-face or by telephone were considered as successfully followed up. We were able to obtain at least some information on all but 7 of our original 407. The hard-to-locate subjects, those who refused to grant a second interview, and those who had died proved no more likely to have relapsed than did the others. In this study, death was more closely correlated with advanced age at first contact than with any other single factor, an observation so obvious that it may escape mention. We have information on 9 of the 15 refusals, 8 of whom were probably sober after the initial interview. Of the 7 who could not be found at all, 5 were women, 4 of them nurses.

Thirty-five subjects died before they were due for a reinterview, 2 so soon and unexpectedly after the first contact that a follow-up interview with the surviving spouse seemed pointless. For 13, interviews were obtained with a significant person fully conversant with the subject's history since the first contact, usually the spouse. For 22 others, no appropriate person could be identified or the interview was refused.

Four-fifths of the subjects reinterviewed reported complete abstinence during the entire follow-up period. Of those who relapsed, 27 drank on only four or fewer occasions, on average less than once a year. Another 46 drank on five or more occasions; however, all but 17 of the surviving subjects had been abstinent for at least two months prior to their reinterview, many for several years.

Only one respondent, a physician whose long-standing drinking history would satisfy the most exacting criteria for alcoholism and who had remained abstinent in A.A. for six years before his initial interview, seems to have successfully returned to "social drinking." He no longer attended A.A., now drank only with his wife, had exchanged a demanding private practice for a fixed-income situation, and had experienced no difficulty related to his resumed drinking over at least a four-year period.

At first interview, 37 percent of the men and 35 percent of the women gave a history of *addiction* to one or more drugs in addition to alcohol. At follow-up, 48 percent of the men and 56 percent of the women acknowledged some drug use during the interval, with 22 percent of each sex still reporting some current use.

At the initial interview, 21 percent of the three medical groups, the only ones asked this question, said that they were currently using one or more mood-altering drugs. None felt themselves to be addicted at that time. Fifty-one men and 26 women did use potentially addicting drugs outside of hospitals during the follow-up period. Of this group, 30 men and 16 women went on to experience difficulties and 18 of these 46 also relapsed into drinking—many using both other drugs and alcohol at the same time. Half of these 46 had been hospitalized for alcohol or drug problems between interviews. Twenty initially reported addiction to nonnarcotic prescription drugs. Ten of these women and 8 men had also reported suicide attempts prior to the first interview. They reported no additional attempts, but three died before the second interview. The experiences of our subjects seem to confirm that the use of other mood-changing drugs by alcoholics carries with it significant danger.

While overt suicide attempts prior to the initial interview were frequent for all subjects, not just those with other addictions, in the interval between interviews only three women and one man made another attempt. One succeeded. While 49 percent of the men and 19 percent of the women reported arrests prior to the initial interview, only six men and three women were arrested during the period between interviews.

Prior to the first interview, the 407 subjects combined had accounted for 3.8 alcohol-related admissions per subject. During the follow-up period, only 1.1 admissions per subject for *all* reasons were reported, and some do not represent ill health. Only 16 percent of these hospitalizations were for alcoholism or other drug-related problems. When abstinence was maintained, suicide attempts, arrests, and hospitalizations markedly decreased.

The following factors in the initial interview appear to be associated with relapses by the 46 who drank five or more days between the interviews: by profession, physicians; those whose parents, especially fathers, were *not* reported to be alcoholics; and a history of other drug problems at the time of initial interview. Attitudes or opinions directly related to relapses were: wanting to return to drinking if it could be done safely; thinking that an alcoholic can return safely to normal drinking; and regarding alcoholism as primarily mental, emotional, or psychological in etiology rather than physical.

Subjects in the initial interview who reported having relapsed after their first year in A.A. were most likely to do so again between the interviews. Relapses were also inversely related to years of sobriety and to chronological age. However, drinking between interviews did *not* vary appreciably according to either reported A.A. attendance or professional treatment before the initial interview.

Addressing the Problem

THE PROFESSIONAL AS A MEMBER OF A.A.

Various support groups limited to professionals have developed both parallel to and within A.A. Most do not attempt to compete with or replace A.A. Of our subjects, for example, 76 percent of the physicians and 55 percent of the dentists belonged to International Doctors in A.A., but were almost always members of regular groups as well.

There was little change in patterns of A.A. attendance over the years between interviews, which probably reflects the fact that the median length of sobriety for the entire sample was already six years at initial interview and that fairly stable habit patterns had already developed. Other attitudes and behaviors also remained rather static. At first interview, 73 percent—and, at reinterview, 74 percent—reported serving alcohol in their homes, while the 35 percent spending two-fifths or less of their social time with other A.A. members rose only to 43 percent. The 26 percent stating that they would drink again if able to do so safely when initially asked became 23 percent of those asked again.

With time, subjects had become a bit more open about their histories. Most families and co-workers were already aware of the subjects' alcoholism at first interview, but only 55 percent thought then that the general public knew. By second interview, 87 percent of the men and 90 percent of the women felt the general public knew.

Professionals have some unique problems in affiliating with A.A., some of their own making and some the result of A.A.'s mores. Groups such as International Doctors in A.A., the British Doctors Group, and International Lawyers in A.A. assist in easing the process of adjustment.

ORGANIZATIONAL RESPONSES

Starting in the early 1970s, the national organizations representing our five professional study groups have been addressing the problem of alcoholism among their members. The American Medical Association (AMA), American Nursing Association (ANA), and National Association of Social Workers (NASW) all have official policy statements. While the American Dental Association (ADA), American Osteopathic Association (AOA), and American Bar Association (ABA) thus far do not, both organized dentistry and osteopathic medicine have nonetheless acted. ADA, as well as AMA, provide model legislation for state-level intervention efforts.

All 50 states now claim to have some sort of impaired physician committee and about 20 states or regional societies have programs for dentists. Nursing has less than 10 currently operational state-level systems, but about 25 states either have started or are actively discussing doing so. No accurate listing of bar association activity is available, but as many as half of the states probably have programs. Some individual Canadian provinces have quite vigorous programs both for physicians and attorneys, although there has been little formal action on a national level. Beyond the initial statement of policy or assignment of a committee or task force to study the matter, neither the AOA nor NASW has made its intent operational.

Many groups of concerned professionals, such as Lawyers Concerned for Lawyers and Social Workers Helping Social Workers, have developed to assist peers directly and to help their organizations. The activities of these groups are described, and contact information is given in Appendix C.

THE RESPONSE OF OTHER PROFESSIONS

Many other professions whose members we did not study have also responded to their alcoholic members. The first groups to do so were Catholic and Episcopal clergy. Pharmacy has a national policy statement and some state-level committees. Psychology does not, but has a committee charged with developing a proposal for the American Psychological Association Board. Veterinary medicine, the organizations representing educators, and the American Library Association have taken no formal action.

The various professions are responding at different paces and with different styles. While all share a common problem, each profession has unique considerations. Most have some sort of self-help or support groups available to members. The responses and special characteristics of these professions are described.

RECOMMENDATIONS FOR ACTION

The professions are faced with the need both to protect the public and to help their colleagues unable to recognize and address their own problems. Compassion and concern for patients and clients, plus awareness of the risk of litigation if one does not act when aware of a present danger, have together generated a growing optimism that something useful can be done. The successful recovery of many professionals both within and outside of A.A. has provided a cadre of concerned individuals insistent that their colleagues receive prompt and appropriate treatment. Necessary legislation has been designed and techniques developed that permit the offering of guidelines for intervention.

While we may not know how to enact primary prevention, secondary prevention for alcoholism and other drug dependencies now takes the form of employee assistance programs and a variety of committees for impaired professionals. Since denial is very much a part of the problem, individual alcoholics must be persuaded or coerced into treatment. A range of intervention approaches is needed with different degrees of available "clout."

Groups that guarantee confidentiality, such as Dentists Concerned for Dentists, Lawyers Concerned for Lawyers, and the A.A. groups, are necessary to serve alcoholics in early stages of the disease at which point their behavior is not yet severe enough to warrant coercive means. For those who cannot or will not be persuaded to see a real problem, other approaches must be used. Since one is forcing a colleague into treatment he or she does not want and since this raises serious concerns about possible violations of civil liberties, every effort must be made to avoid conflict of interest, inappropriate treatment, or any question that the rescuer is in any way self-serving. And there is a related problem. Although we may be well aware that an early drinking problem once visible will in all likelihood get worse, one is simply not able, even if certain it would be desirable, to bring a coercive mechanism into play, since alcoholism is difficult to prove. There are too many issues of due process and the subtle evidence of something different about a certain individual's drinking behavior that is impossible to describe, especially if this evidence must hold up in court or at a professional board hearing.

Ideally, the alcoholic professional should be treated—and treated early rather than punished. If this is done skillfully, formal sanctions such as banishment from a hospital staff or loss of license need never occur. Harm to colleagues, family, and patients or clients can be averted.

In the past, as our research subjects clearly demonstrate, action by peers often came very late, if it came at all. The public will probably very easily accept that professionals are not immune to the ills that affect everyone else, if we agree to acknowledge a problem and deal with it.

ONE | The Study

2

Prevalence and Procedures

Although the problem of drug dependence in our society is receiving increased public and professional attention, specific information about alcoholism in the professions is still relatively scarce. It is a matter of growing concern in those occupations where professionals have direct responsibility not only to themselves and their families, but to others as well. Members of a profession not only share a specialized body of knowledge but also subscribe to a code of ethics that tacitly recognizes special privilege and with it the capacity to harm patients or clients if it is abused. This book presents the first data available on a substantial number of alcoholics in five high-status occupations and it is the first longitudinal study of both male and female A.A. members.

The vast majority of what has been written to date concerning the highly educated or professional person has been about the physician. There are many newspaper accounts of the drug and alcohol problems of individual celebrities, but most of these are politicians, sports figures, entertainers, or authors, some of whom are incidentally professionals as well. If therefore we seem to slight other professions in favor of medicine, it is primarily because of the relative lack of available information.

PREVALENCE

There are still no reliable studies of the prevalence of alcoholism among the members of professional groups. While disciplinary bodies, impaired physician committees, and advocacy groups such as Lawyers Concerned for Lawyers may report on the number of cases brought to their attention, neither they nor we know how many others remain hidden.

Since alcoholism is a disease whose hallmark is denial on the part of the alcoholic and by family, friends, and colleagues as well, its presence is acknowledged late, if at all. Those most closely involved are often the last to recognize it in themselves or others.

As each professional group begins to examine its own behavior, there is often an initial assumption that intelligence and professional education alone can protect against alcoholism and that the problem, while present, is probably uncommon. With a closer look and growing sophistication, this may then change to the counterclaim that "role strain" or the stresses and life-style supposedly typical of the practice of law or health care may actually lead to even greater risk than that faced by those in other professions. Both postures are based more on opinion than evidence.

We do know something about factors that correlate with high rates of alcoholism in the general population and this permits us to make some educated guesses about what is likely to be found in special populations. If we assume that professionals are at the same risk as other Americans, then roughly 1 in 10 of the adult male professionals who drink and 1 in 20 of the females will be alcoholic or experience a serious drinking problem (1). If we then examine professions like medicine, law, and dentistry, where men predominate, rates should be higher than in nursing or social work simply because, in spite of the narrowing gender gap both in alcoholism and in career choice, there are still more alcoholic men than women.

Relative affluence, exposure to the sophisticated environment of urban areas, distancing from the more abstinence-oriented fundamentalist religions, social settings in which drinking is accepted, very high (as well as very low) educational level—all of these variables have been associated with higher rates of drinking and thus the possibility of accompanying problems (2,3).

Whatever protection the members of a profession may derive from training and information or from the fact of their having successfully passed through a screening process before admission to school or practice may well be counterbalanced by other factors that actually increase the chance of trouble. It was surprisingly easy for us to locate large numbers of recovered alcoholic professionals when they were sought, which may imply the existence of a very large pool both of those still drinking and of those who have stopped.

Just as there is little solid data on the prevalence of alcoholism in the professions, so too is there a relative paucity of information on the outcome of treatment. Most reports are from treatment facilities whose patient populations are not chosen by any criteria that would permit identification of untreated control groups or groups treated in different ways (4). Results are too often reported after very short follow-up periods, which is obviously less than ideal for a relapsing illness. There is only rarely an attempt even to compare professional groups with each other or with other patients in the same treatment setting (5,6). And it is self-evident that most treatment facilities are less likely to issue reports of failure than they are to present their efforts in the best possible light. How an author describes his or her patients reflects the author's background and orientation. Psychiatric hospitals, for example, will sometimes routinely assign an additional psychiatric diagnosis to each alcoholic patient (7). The idea that an alcoholic patient may not be emotionally ill is not even entertained. Women, except in those professions that are almost entirely made up of women, are rather consistently excluded from study, just as male nurses may be ignored.

Attempts to estimate the prevalence of alcoholism in the professions are few in number and of questionable validity. Most of what has been written concerns physicians and nurses rather than the other professions. In the discussion that follows and in our selection of references, we will appear to be giving a disproportionate amount of attention to medical professionals. This is not to imply that they are of any greater interest or importance than the others, but simply reflects the relative lack of available information on the other groups.

In fact, any human condition that carries with it a great deal of social stigma or is regarded as intensely personal in nature is hard to measure, particularly when it is fairly easily concealed. Obesity and skin color are visible; life-style and behavior much less so. Thus the difficulty of detection also contributes to the scanty literature available on alcoholism but explains perhaps why the medical profession, since it is so much in the public eye, predominates the literature.

Currently available statistics are based on one or more of the following procedures:

1. Estimates are made to examine risk factors for alcoholism in the population at large; then a search is conducted for their presence in the population under discussion to arrive at what is ultimately an educated guess.

2. Reports of disciplinary bodies such as licensing boards and court records are examined. These are inevitably underestimates since by no means are all cases brought to the attention of these bodies and many that are investigated lack sufficient documentation to warrant diagnosis and subsequent reporting. (See Table 4.1.)

3. The proportion of people in a treatment population who are members of a given profession are studied. Their numbers are then compared with their proportion in the general population to see if they are overrepresented or underrepresented. This assumes that all alcoholics have an equal likelihood of finding their way into a particular treatment setting.

4. Prevalence of a condition known to be associated with heavy drinking, such as cirrhosis of the liver, is the point of departure. If there is a great deal of cirrhosis, one then assumes the population contains a great deal of alcoholism as well.

5. Responses to questionnaires and other survey instruments are used, usually allowing the respondent to remain anonymous. Results depend on the willingness of those surveyed to respond, their veracity, their sophistication, and their degree of denial. Those surveyed may be randomly selected or, as in the present study, may be those likely to be particularly interested in and sensitized to the presence of alcoholism in peers.

The claim is common that physicians must have an unusually high prevalence of alcoholism because they make up a disproportionately large percentage of patients seeking psychiatric help or found in psychiatric hospitals (8,9,10). Similar statements have been made about nurses. Glatt, for example, noted that 35 of 450 female alcoholics admitted to St. Bernard's Hospital (1958–67) were nurses (11,12,13). A Scottish study showed the first admission rate for alcohol dependence among physicians was 2.7 times higher than controls in the same social class (14).

The case for more alcoholism among physicians is bolstered by studies showing them to have a high mortality rate from cirrhosis of the liver—3.5 times that of the general population in Great Britain. Cook, however, argues that the high rate is not necessarily the result of alcoholism, since the high risk of hepatitis, especially hepatitis B, could be partly responsible (15). With the current knowledge of immunology, this particular argument could now be investigated and resolved.

Our own study suggests quite another explanation for the discovery of so many alcoholic doctors and nurses in treatment. Our physicians were treated as hospital patients and sought help from psychiatrists much more often than all the other professional groups. Nurses did so almost as often, while equally affluent dentists, attorneys, and college women did not.

We asked at first interview whether a subject had had cirrhosis or fatty liver, but these illnesses were not described and appeared on a checklist. These terms would have a different meaning to health-care and lay groups, and one can never trust that even physician-patients are fully informed about their own health. Eight percent of the three health-care groups reported having cirrhosis and 15 percent fatty liver, compared to 5 percent and 20 percent in the non-health-care groups. Only the nurses appeared at particular risk since they represent 10 of the 12 women reporting cirrhosis. Twelve percent of those addicted to narcotics as well as alcohol reported cirrhosis versus 6 percent of those who did not inject narcotics. But these numbers are too small to suggest more than the need for more investigation, particularly since there is little reason for physicians, nurses, and dentists to use unsterile needles.

We asked our research subjects about their own awareness of other colleagues in trouble at the time of the first interview. The question not only was carefully worded but was repeated by the interviewer to make certain that we were asking about those currently in trouble, rather than those known in the past, and that there was no need for certainty about the diagnosis. (A.A. members are often very reluctant to "take someone else's inventory" or label someone else as alcoholic. A.A. philosophy insists that each member should decide for himself or herself whether or not he or she is alcoholic.) We asked, "How many other nurses [or attorneys, or dentists, etc.] are *presently* known to you whom you are reasonably certain have a serious drinking problem?"

Since some of the women were working as homemakers rather than at a profession and others were not in hospital or agency settings, and since some attorneys worked in banks or insurance companies rather than with other lawyers, many explained that they would have little opportunity to know of others. A few other individuals were working full time in an alcoholism treatment center, so were made aware of many more. So too were some individuals serving on committees or who were part of advocacy groups designed to work with peers. (We did not ask the physicians this particular question in the first interview.) Our average subject—in all of the professional groups—was aware of four others currently in trouble with alcohol.

How large is the problem of alcoholism in the professions? According to the U.S. Bureau of the Census (16), there were, in 1981, 454,000 physicians (medical doctors and osteopaths), 130,000 dentists, 581,000 lawyers, 1,339,000 registered nurses, 152,000 pharmacists, and as many as 511,000 social workers, if one includes those without a master's degree. These groups alone represent over 3 million people and do not include many other professionals who should probably be listed, such as veterinarians and psychologists. If we accept that 9 percent of male drinkers and 5 percent of female drinkers are at substantial risk of developing alcoholism or a serious drinking problem (1), and further assume that only 70 percent of our professionals drink (a deliberately low estimate) and that half of the 2.2 million drinkers listed above are women, then these groups alone should contain more than 150,000 who are or will be in trouble with alcohol.

In its 1980 survey, A.A. reports that, of its 24,950 membership sample, 17 percent of the men and 18 percent of the women described their present employment as "professional" but no further details are available (17). There are many more people now in all of the helping professions compared to when our study first began.

If we look at the dentists alone, there were already 108,000 during the study years. In 1972 (16), assuming that 8 percent of this largely male group were alcoholic, there should have been about

9,000 in the United States. If it is also true, as the National Institute on Alcohol Abuse and Alcoholism stated in 1978, that only 10 percent of alcoholics find their way into A.A. or into treatment (18), then there should have been only about 900 who either had received treatment or were A.A. members abstinent for a full year. To locate 49 of them for interviewing, more than 5 percent of all the available recovered alcoholic dentists in A.A., should have been almost an impossible task. It was not.

The same held true for the other professions. Only psychologists have been difficult to locate within A.A. Are A.A. members less anonymous and more available than has been assumed? Are there many more alcoholic professionals than we even suspected? Have greater numbers joined A.A. than we thought possible? Unfortunately, these can only be questions of conjecture. Acceptable subjects were found to be quite available when we began our study. Many times the number we studied could easily be found today. Even if inclined to minimize the magnitude of the problem, most physicians, and probably those in the other professions as well, are usually aware of at least one colleague who may be alcohol or drug dependent. (If someone is under the influence of a sedative drug, it may be impossible to tell by observation if the particular drug is alcohol, a minor tranquilizer, or a soporific.) Most continue to be reluctant to take action.

In an attempt to determine type and prevalence of physician impairment, the Florida Medical Association Auxiliary late in 1979 mailed 4,000 questionnaires to its members. The return rate of 18 percent (700 respondents) is poor, and the study's validity therefore is questionable (19). Perhaps the poor response is because of the highly personal nature of the questions asked. In any event, to the question, "In your own community are you or your spouse aware of a physician suffering from an impairment due to abuse of alcohol or other drugs?": 63 percent answered yes; 34 percent, no; and 3 percent did not answer. They were asked to choose between several possible responses to "If your husband is aware of a colleague's excessive use of alcohol and other drugs what has he done about it?" Some 28 percent denied knowing anyone in the community suffering with the problem (sometimes adding "at this time"); but 31 percent said, "Did nothing"; 25 percent, "Personally tried to help"; 2 percent, "Avoided him completely"; and only 3 percent reported the situation to a medical board. Comments

from two wives about their own husband's situation were "I do not
know where to turn without exposing the situation badly," and "I
agonize and wait for a colleague to notice and come to me lest I be
accused of betrayal."

Niven asked 1,000 physicians enrolled in continuing medical
education courses at the Mayo Clinic about their awareness of
alcoholism in colleagues and what they would do about it (20). Of
the 784 respondents, 91 percent were family practitioners and most
were from the Midwest. Niven concluded that they were better at
recognizing the symptoms than in addressing the problem. Most
were indeed aware of a colleague with a "serious psychiatric or
chemical dependency problem," but many also expressed reluctance to take action unless the ability to practice was seriously
impaired, and some not even then. Many were pessimistic about
rehabilitation and would be reluctant to practice with a physician
recovering from alcoholism, although as many would be willing
to do this as would be willing to practice with a physician
recently recovered from an episode of psychotic depression.

After a rather exhaustive literature review, we simply cannot
now say with any degree of certainty how many members of any
major profession already are or will become alcoholic. There are,
to be sure, relevant statements that sound firm and authoritative,
but if one pursues references and examines the available data, one
can only echo the executive director of a major professional
organization who wrote back to us, "We just don't know, Doctor,
we just don't know."

EFFECTS ON PROFESSIONALS

Many health-care professionals know little or nothing about the
early recognition of alcoholism, and as treaters themselves they
may be unusually slow to seek help or to assume the patient role.
When the search for help does begin, it often leads to a friend or
colleague no better prepared to deal with the problem. Inappropriate treatment and long delays in intervention have been more
the rule than the exception (21).

Alcoholism, once a certain number of indicators are present,
manifests itself as a progressive illness with periods of remission
and exacerbation (22). It may appear to remain static for months
or years but usually gets steadily and slowly worse with the

passage of time. Without some abrupt change or dramatic event, people tend to postpone action. Even when unpleasant, there is comfort in the familiar. Meanwhile, other difficulties may progressively appear. Usually family relationships are the first to be disrupted, then other social patterns. Minor accidents, financial indiscretions, and health problems occur. Only much later, if at all, are there arrests or obvious interference with work. A career or practice, in fact, are often the last to go. The ability to reassure oneself that no patient or client was hurt is grimly defended and believed to be true. The ability to work and care for others proves that one still has value and is needed, that things can't really be too bad so long as one still can function as a professional.

EFFECTS ON PATIENTS

While we cannot know in detail how much harm is actually done to patients or clients by the alcoholic or drug-using professional, it must be significant. Trying to work with a hangover or just not feeling well much of the time has an influence (23). Long before serious mistakes of technique or judgment are made, there will be many journals not read and many lectures only half heard. While drinking itself demands time and attention, alters mood and thought processes, and has its other physical effects (24) distractions caused by family upsets and secondary problems also can interfere with work. Even when a performance is not really bad, in a host of subtle ways the excellence a professional is capable of is stripped away. It is relatively simple to recognize a colleague who is frankly drunk and to prevent that person from mounting the judge's bench, accepting the key to the drug cupboard, or doing surgery, but the implications of heavy "social" drinking at lunch before perhaps seeing medical students or evaluating patients in the afternoon, when behavior deviates only slightly from the norm, are much harder to judge.

PROFESSIONAL RESPONSE

In general, professional intervention still takes place quite late in a drinking career, and even then only when some other agency has first become involved. Classically, the alcoholic nurse will be ignored unless she also becomes involved with narcotics and is discovered stealing drugs. Law enforcement personnel and state bodies then enter the picture. This happens with physicians as well. If someone is convicted of a felony, the license to practice is placed in jeopardy and colleagues can no longer look aside. At this point one may discover that there have been months and years of warning signs—repeated hospitalizations, arrests for driving while intoxicated, stormy divorces, even suicide attempts— all ignored. The general delay in expressions of concern by peers is changing rapidly, and some groups, particularly in law and medicine, are leading the way.

DRUGS

Many alcoholics attempt to decrease their drinking by substituting other mood-changing drugs, usually sedatives and tranquilizers. Most are limited in the choice of drugs by problems of availability. This is not true in health care, where the nurse, dentist, and physician can obtain a variety of agents, including narcotics, without becoming involved in the illicit drug culture or learning to manage on the street. While we found in our study that the difference in the numbers of alcoholics within the medical and the nonmedical professions who reported addiction to another drug in addition to alcohol was not very substantial (39 percent and 32 percent, respectively), the type of drug varied. Physicians and nurses do report addiction to narcotics more often than lawyers and educated women. This difference adds a special problem for these professionals, but also sometimes provides their colleagues with an additional means of detection as well as the added ability to use the law in order to coerce the alcoholic into treatment.

OUR STUDY

In order to learn more about alcoholism among both medical and nonmedical professionals, we studied 407 persons in selected high-status occupations: physicians, dentists, nurses, attorneys, social workers, and college-educated women in other fields.

All subjects described themselves as alcoholics and as A.A. members, and had reportedly done no drinking whatsoever for at least one year immediately before the initial interview. The same subjects were reinterviewed five to seven years after their first interview, with a follow-up rate of almost 90 percent. All of these interviews were conducted face-to-face with the subjects by staff, who were themselves recovered alcoholics. If a subject was no longer living, we attempted to interview his or her next of kin. We used a structured questionnaire that differed for each of the two conducted interviews and differed among professions as appropriate.

The minimum of one year's continuous sobriety at the time of the initial interview was required so that subjects might more accurately recall and report past events in their lives. (It is doubtful that most alcoholics can accurately remember and report personal events while they are fresh from drinking, perhaps still organic or in the denial phase, or not yet comfortable with and willing to share their own history.) We chose to interview only A.A. members since other recovered alcoholics who are not in A.A. are much more difficult to identify, locate, and interview.

Potential respondents were first identified with the help of other individual A.A. members, at meetings for specific professions, such as International Doctors in A.A. (a group limited to doctoral level health-care professionals, mostly physicians and dentists), or through alcoholism treatment facilities. Since subjects were approached only after they had first given friends, colleagues, or treatment staff permission for us to make contact, some reports that potential subjects were away on vacation or ill may represent refusals to be interviewed. Thus, all of the respondents were invited to participate in the study. There were virtually no volunteers and very few refusals—either explicit or implicit.

A consequence of this identification process was that the more active and visible A.A. members are probably overrepresented in our sample. In addition, most of the subjects lived in larger urban areas since more time and money were necessary for us to pursue interviews in small towns and rural areas. Many interviews took place during meetings and conventions. Thus, it must be emphasized that the sample is not random, not self-selected, nor necessarily representative of recovered alcoholics in the selected professions who would meet the other study criteria. The subjects are instead a *purposive* sample with specified qualifications.

SAMPLE DESCRIPTION

The total sample consists of 214 men and 193 women. All of the 97 physicians and 49 dentists, 49 of 55 attorneys, and 19 of 50 social workers are men, as indicated in Table 2.1. All of the 100 registered nurses, 31 of the social workers, and 6 attorneys are women, and there are 56 other women of comparable education. Thus, two of the professional groups are completely male, two are completely female, one is almost all male, and one is 62 percent female.

The physicians, dentists, registered nurses, and attorneys had all received the degrees required to practice their professions; the social workers all had earned a master's degree in social work. In the group of college women, all subjects had completed a minimum of three years' college; three-fifths (61%) of them had earned at least a bachelor's degree, and some had advanced degrees as well. None were living with medical professionals or working in health-care settings. Many worked as teachers or in publishing.

Perhaps this is a good place to say a word about these college women. As a group, they were very diversified. Most lived in and were interviewed in New York, San Francisco, or Chicago. While all had to have completed at least three years of education beyond high school, most had a bachelor's degree and quite a few also had a master's degree or doctorate degree. (An early attempt in the study to interview licensed practical nurses had revealed that our questionnaire was too sophisticated to work well with all members of such a group where educational levels varied so widely and were, in some cases, quite limited.) We found that many of the college women were employed in publishing, many as editors. Others were teachers. Two ran small businesses. Two were artists. Some are currently homemakers. Our intent was not to pretend to have surveyed a representative sample of educated women but, instead, to learn if women employed in hospital settings or in the helping professions would prove to differ sharply from those in other fields, particularly in matters such as use of drugs other than alcohol and in their manner of seeking help.

Overall, reinterviews were obtained for 362 of the 407 subjects (89%) five to seven years after the original interview, as shown in Table 2.1. These include in-person reinterviews with 350 subjects

Table 2.1 Selected Study Data According to Profession

	All Subjects (407)	Profession					
N =		Physicians (97)	Dentists (49)	Nurses (100)	Attorneys (55)	Social Workers (50)	College Women (56)
Sex							
Men (%)	53	100	100	—	89	38	—
Women (%)	47	—	—	100	11	62	100
Age (at first interview)							
Median age (years)	48	51	53	47	49	44	46
Range (years)							
Youngest	26	36	37	26	31	26	28
Oldest	74	74	70	69	72	66	64
Follow-up rate (%)	89	94	84	87	87	84	95

33

and 12 next of kin when the subject was deceased. The follow-up rate ranged from 84 percent for the dentists and social workers to about 95 percent for the physicians and college women. There was very little difference in the follow-up rates for men and women. Even for those for whom next of kin could not be interviewed, we were able to obtain at least some information. Only seven had completely vanished. (See Table 6.1.)

The men in our study were somewhat older than the women; their median ages when first interviewed were 51 and 46, respectively. One-half of the men compared to one-third of the women reported that their present religion was Protestant, while about 30 percent of both sexes were Catholic. There were only 16 Jewish respondents (9 men and 7 women). More than twice as many women as men claimed no present religious affiliation (22% and 10%, respectively).

Since the males in the study were in predominantly male professions, and the women in predominantly female professions, it is not surprising that a much larger proportion of the men than women were in the same profession as were their fathers. On the other hand, a slightly larger proportion of female subjects than male subjects had fathers who were professionals. One-sixth of the men and only 3 percent of the women had the same occupations as their fathers. However, the fathers of one-quarter of the women and one-fifth of the men were professionals in other occupations. We did not ask about the mother's occupation.

There was no particular gender difference in the high educational achievements typical of these respondents. About one-fifth of both men and women were Phi Beta Kappa or had received honors in college, and more than three-fifths of both sexes reported graduating in the top third of their professional school class.

Although many more men than women had been on active duty in the military services, the number of women with previous active military service was also relatively large, and 23 of these 25 were nurses. What is most significant, however, is that more than 1 in 10 of both the men and women with military service received other than honorable discharges (11%, men; 12%, women). We did not ask the reasons and cannot say with certainty that alcohol was in any way involved.

At the time of the original interview, most of the subjects were in their forties (36%) or fifties (27%), with 17 percent in their thirties and 16 percent in their sixties. Only 2 percent were under thirty and 2 percent were over 70. The overall median age at the time of the first interview was 48 (Table 2.1). The median for physicians and dentists was over 50 years of age, and only the social workers had a median age under 45.

Almost all the subjects were white (97%) and born in the United States (94%). Five of the lawyers, two physicians, two dentists, two nurses, and two social workers were black. One social worker was Hispanic. Most of the 25 foreign-born subjects were Canadians (76%), and all of these were from English-speaking backgrounds.

Three-fifths of all subjects were married (59%); of the remainder, equal numbers had never married (18%) or were divorced (17%). Since more than twice as many men (80%) as women (36%) were married at the time of the first interview, this is reflected in the proportion in each profession who were married.

Women alcoholics are more likely to be divorced than their male counterparts (25,26). These findings are supported by the reports of our subjects. Almost one-third of the women had never been married, while in contrast four-fifths of the men were married at the time of the initial interview. The married men and women in our study seemed about equally likely to have had more than one spouse. The men were somewhat more likely than were the women to have had children.

The men in our study reported more years of sobriety than did the women, perhaps reflecting their five-year median age difference. While the women attended A.A. meetings somewhat more often, there was no appreciable sex difference in participation in A.A. activities, nor was there any particular difference in the number of reported relapses or "slips" since first attending an A.A. meeting. More than half of both sexes reported no subsequent drinking after their first A.A. meeting, and another one-fifth reported none after their first year in A.A.

THE QUESTIONNAIRE

The topics in the first interview included the subject's background; the drinking history and eight "benchmarks"; use of other mood-altering drugs and addiction; experiences related to drinking, including signs and symptoms of alcoholism; high-risk behaviors including overdoses and suicide attempts; professional or legal sanctions related to drinking; treatment and A.A. experiences; familial alcoholism; and alcohol-related attitudes or opinions. The topics in the second (follow-up) interview included sobriety or relapses, other drug use, related problems or changes, as well as experiences in the period between interviews. Abridged interview items are presented in Appendix A.

Background topics included demographic characteristics and educational, occupational, and income data. Subjects' drinking experiences included blackouts, loss of control, regular morning drinking, loss of alcohol tolerance, liver disease, and other health complications. Some experiences were recorded by respondents on a checklist. All other information was obtained from answers to standardized questions.

The eight "benchmarks" are important milestones in the drinking history of alcoholics. The age of the subjects when these key drinking experiences first occurred was obtained by asking, "At what age or in what year did the following occur":

- You first became concerned about your drinking?
- You started drinking with some regularity?
- Drinking first began to interfere with your life?
- You first got drunk?
- You began getting drunk with some regularity?
- Someone else first expressed concern to you about your drinking?
- You went to an A.A. meeting?
- You had your very last drink?

CLASSIFYING SUBJECTS

In the following chapters, we will be looking at similarities and differences in the progression of alcoholism and recovery in five specific professions and a group of college-educated women, comparing medical and nonmedical professionals, men and women, and the various respondents according to their addiction to drugs other than alcohol. The use of mood-altering drugs other than alcohol may be an important factor in the course of alcoholism and recovery, and physicians and nurses have relatively easier access to other mood-altering drugs, particularly narcotics, than do other professionals with equivalent educational backgrounds.

Physicians and other health professionals may also be better qualified to report accurately on the physical consequences of their alcoholism and on their use of treatment resources.

Respondents were classified according to whether or not they had in the first interview reported ever being addicted to non-narcotic mood-altering drugs or to narcotics. Almost all of the respondents reporting a history of addiction to narcotics stated that they had been addicted to other mood-altering drugs as well. Thus, we classified them into three "addiction groups": alcohol alone; alcohol plus nonnarcotic drugs; and alcohol plus narcotics, with or without addiction to nonnarcotics. In the first interview, subjects in the alcohol plus narcotics group reported addiction to "hard" drugs, such as morphine, heroin, or Demerol. The 12 subjects addicted to "soft" narcotics, such as codeine or Percodan, but not to "hard" drugs, were included in the alcohol plus non-narcotics group. Nine of these 12 reported addiction to nonnar-cotics as well. We thought it best to exclude physicians' wives and hospital workers from the college women group because of the possibility of their own easier access to other drugs. We were alert to social workers who might have worked at hospitals during their drinking years, but this did not present a problem.

REFERENCES

1. National Institute on Alcohol Abuse and Alcoholism, *Fourth Special Report to the U.S. Congress on Alcohol and Health*, Washington, D.C.: Department of Health and Human Services, 1981.

2. H. A. Mulford, "The Epidemiology of Alcoholism and Its Implications," in: *Encyclopedic Handbook of Alcoholism*, E. M. Pattison and E. Kaufman, eds., New York: Gardner Press, 1982, pp. 441–57.

3. D. B. Heath, "Sociocultural Variants in Alcoholism," ibid., pp. 426–40.

4. M. J. Goby et al., "Physicians Treated for Alcoholism: A Follow-Up Study," *Alcoholism: Clinical and Experimental Research 3*: 1979, pp. 121–24.

5. J. Spicer et al., *Characteristics and Outcomes of Professionals Admitted to the Hazelden Rehabilitation Center, 1973–1976*, Center City, Minn.: Hazelden, 1978.

6. R. A. Franklin, "One Hundred Doctors at the Retreat," *British Journal of Psychiatry 131*: 1977, pp. 11–14.

7. R. P. Johnson and J. C. Connelly, "Addicted Physicians, A Closer Look," *Journal of the American Medical Association 245*: January 15, 1981, pp. 253–57.

8. J. C. Duffy and E. M. Litin, *The Emotional Health of Physicians*, Springfield, Ill.: Charles C Thomas, 1967.

9. H. C. Modlin and A. Montes, "Narcotics Addiction in Physicians," *American Journal of Psychiatry 121*: 1964, pp. 358–63.

10. R. E. Jones, "Do Psychiatrists Cover up Addiction of Physicians?" *Psychiatric Opinion 12*: 1975, pp. 31–36.

11. M. M. Glatt, "Alcoholism and Drug Dependence in Doctors and Nurses," *British Medical Journal*, February 10, 1968, pp. 380–81.

12. ———, "Alcoholism an Occupational Hazard for Doctors," *Journal of Alcoholism 11*: 1976, pp. 85–91.

13. ———, "Characteristics and Prognosis of Alcoholic Doctors" (letter), *British Medical Journal*, February 19, 1977, p. 507.

14. P. M. Murray, "Alcoholism among Male Doctors in Scotland," *Lancet*, October 2, 1976, pp. 729–31.

15. P. Cook, "Cirrhosis in Doctors," *Lancet*, January 20, 1979, p. 156.

16. U.S. Bureau of the Census, *Statistical Abstract of the United States: 1982–83* (103rd edition), Washington, D.C.: 1982, p. 338.

17. "Analysis of the 1980 Survey of the Membership of A.A." (unpublished), New York: Alcoholics Anonymous, 1980.

18. National Institute on Alcohol Abuse and Alcoholism, *Third Special Report to the U.S. Congress on Alcohol and Health* (Technical Support Document), Washington, D.C.: Department of Health and Human Services, June 1978, p. xxi.

19. M. Weigand, "The Florida Physician and His Family in Crisis," *Journal of the Florida Medical Association 68*: 1981, pp. 195–99.

20. R. G. Niven, "Physicians Perceptions and Attitudes Toward Disabled Colleagues," in: *The Impaired Physician, Proceedings of the Third Annual Conference on the Impaired Physician*, Minneapolis, 1978, Chicago: Department of Mental Health, American Medical Association, 1980, pp. 21–26.

21. L. Bissell and R. W. Jones, "The Alcoholic Nurse," *Nursing Outlook 29*: February 1981, pp. 96–101.

22. G. E. Vaillant, *The Natural History of Alcoholism*, Cambridge, Mass.: Harvard University Press, 1983.

23. D. H. Franck, "If You Drink Don't Drive Motto Now Applies to Hangovers as Well," *Journal of the American Medical Association 250*: October 7, 1983, pp. 1657–58.

24. D. A. Parker et al., "Alcohol Use and Cognitive Loss among Employed Men and Women," *American Journal of Public Health 73*: 1983, pp. 521–26.

25. P. Kent, *An American Woman and Alcohol*, New York: Holt, Rinehart and Winston, 1967.

26. E. M. Corrigan, *Alcoholic Women in Treatment*, New York: Oxford University Press, 1980.

3

Course of Alcohol and Other Drug Use

Anyone exploring the literature on alcoholism and other drug addiction immediately faces the problem of definition. Some authors regard "addiction" and "alcoholism" as synonymous with physical dependence. Others view any use of a drug that is illegal, self-prescribed, or used in quantities larger than that ordered by a single physician as "misuse" or "drug abuse." The word "abuse" is not only imprecise, but has a rather moralistic and judgmental flavor that limits its usefulness in an interview situation. Sometimes terms are not defined at all, or simply having been in treatment for a drug- or alcohol-related problem is sometimes considered diagnostic of alcoholism or "chemical dependency." (Thus, nonalcoholics arrested for driving while intoxicated have been lumped with alcoholics in reports of federally funded treatment programs, and we are then told that sizable numbers of "alcoholics" are capable of successful social drinking after treatment.)

As stated in Chapter 2, we decided to accept the self-evaluation of our subjects as to their alcoholism and it seems unlikely that many were mistaken. All called themselves alcoholic, had joined A.A., and had given up drinking. The vast majority had to be sought out cautiously with care not to disclose the purpose of the interview to others since there is still much more stigma than status in being identified as alcoholic.

People with a history of addiction to one drug are prone to dependence on other drugs as well. It is also a truism that, when drugs are familiar and easily available, people tend to use them. There are historical accounts not only of addiction in famous individuals like Halstead and Freud but of widespread use of narcotics in physicians and nurses (1,2). Both of these groups are described as overrepresented in drug treatment populations. Physicians found overprescribing for patients often have been addicts themselves (3). Most of these reports of physician and nurse addicts say little about drinking history or its effect on the individual other than to cite alcoholism and chronic pain, fatigue, and stress as fellow travelers.

DRINKING BENCHMARKS

We have chosen the eight previously described benchmarks as key steps in the history of alcoholics from the time that drinking starts with some regularity to the last reported drink. For men and women, regardless of their profession or addiction to other drugs, the sequence and age of onset of the initial benchmarks were very similar. Respondents tended to get drunk for the first time in their late teens, about two years before they started drinking with any regularity. The median age when subjects first drank on a regular basis was 20, whether or not they would also experience being addicted to other drugs (Table 3.1). These early drinking experiences occurred two years earlier for men than for women (regular drinking at median age 19 and 21, respectively).

If this seems a relatively late beginning, keep in mind that almost half (45%) of the respondents were 50 years of age or older when first interviewed and about one-quarter grew up before the Prohibition Amendment was repealed in 1933. People start to drink at a younger age now (4); moreover, Prohibition would have generally delayed the initial drinking of young people of that time. Respondents began getting drunk with some regularity at a median age of 26, regardless of sex or other drug addiction. Thus, five or six years of more moderate drinking were described before the professionals in our study started to get drunk on a regular basis.

It is very difficult to pinpoint the exact onset of a disease that typically is slowly progressive and episodic and shows marked

Table 3.1 Selected Drinking-Related Experiences: Median Age of First Occurrence

Median Age of Onset for Significant Experiences N =	All Subjects (407)	Sex		Addictions[a]		
		Men (214)	Women (193)	Alcohol Only (259)	Alcohol and Nonnarcotics (115)	Alcohol and "Hard" Narcotics (33)
Drinking regularly	20	19	21	20	20	20
Drunk regularly	26	25	26	26	26	25
Drinking interfered with life	29	30	28	30	29	27
First A.A. meeting	40	41	38	40	39	40
Last drink	42	44	40	43	42	41
Time interval between drinking regularly and last drink (years)	22	25	19	23	22	21

[a] The category Alcohol and Nonnarcotics *does not* include any subjects who reported addiction to "hard" narcotics, but *does* include nine subjects who *also* reported addiction to codeine and three who *only* reported addiction to codeine. The category Alcohol and "Hard" Narcotics includes subjects who *also* reported addiction to nonnarcotics or "soft" narcotics.

diversity in the occurrence, frequency, and severity of its related signs or symptoms. Alcoholism, in addition, carries a high degree of social stigma, decreasing the likelihood of its recognition by both the alcoholic and the physician or others who might provide treatment. We can argue that, since genetics plays a part in determining who becomes alcoholic (5,6,7,8), the predisposition could even be regarded as present from birth but simply not perceptible until after a number of years of exposure to alcohol. A.A. members refer to "crossing the invisible boundary line" from normal drinker to alcoholic and see this as a permanent change. A favorite saying is, "Once a cucumber becomes a pickle, it can't go back to being a cucumber." In a much more sophisticated vein, Vaillant notes that individuals who have once demonstrated four or more specific indicators are those unlikely ever to return to drinking successfully (9). Marden argues that alcoholism, like homosexuality, exists on a continuum and that the decision to diagnose at any given point is necessarily arbitrary (10). If there is a moment at which an individual's alcoholism begins, it would not be easy to define it or to get others to agree on it. Nevertheless, several of the drinking benchmarks in our study are useful in identifying in retrospect what might be called the onset of active alcoholism. These are the times when the subject began getting drunk with some regularity, when drinking first began interfering with his or her life, when someone else first expressed concern about the subject's drinking, and when personal concern began.

For men and women in all six groups studied, regardless of other antecedent or subsequent addiction status, these four benchmarks almost without exception occurred in the same order. The typical course was that drinking first began to interfere with respondents' lives about three years after they began getting drunk with some regularity. Two years later someone else first expressed concern, and within the next two years the respondents first became concerned about their own drinking (expressed in median years).

The criterion we prefer to use for the onset of alcoholism is when drinking first begins to interfere with the person's life. This benchmark incorporates most of the components of Keller's often-cited definition of alcoholism: "a chronic disease manifested by repeated implicative drinking so as to cause injury to the drinker's health or to his social or economic functioning" (11). Our benchmark of regular drunkenness seems to correspond to "repeated implicative drinking" and interference in the drinker's life and interference itself as benchmarks seem to correspond to "injury to the drinker's health or to his social or economic functioning."

In a study of A.A. members in New York City, more than 1,000 participants were asked about four drinking-related experiences that are comparable to our benchmarks (12). The average age of onset for these drinking experiences in the New York City study is strikingly similar to our findings (Table 3.2). The similarity of these results is more remarkable in view of the differences between the samples and study designs. Although the average age of the two samples was identical, more than half (54%) of the New York City group had not attended college, a substantial minority had been attending A.A. or were sober for less than one year, and self-administered questionnaires, rather than personal interviews, were used.

Does the onset of alcoholism among professionals precede or follow the completion of their formal education? Physicians, dentists, and attorneys in our study obtained their respective professional degrees at a median age of 27, and in all three groups the subjects felt that drinking first interfered with their lives at a median age of 31. The registered nurses completed their basic training at a much younger age—in their early twenties (median age, 23) and drinking first began interfering with their lives at a

Table 3.2 Onset of Selected Drinking-Related Experiences: Professional Persons and New York City A.A. Members

Drinking-Related Experiences	Average (Mean) Age of First Occurrence	
	Professional Persons (N = 407)	New York City A.A. Members[a] (N = 1023)
Other's concern	32	34
Personal concern	34	36
First A.A. meeting	40	42[b]
Last drink	43	46[c]
Age	49	49

[a]Self-administered interviews. See reference 12.
[b]Including 16 percent in A.A. for less than one year.
[c]Including 37 percent with continuous sobriety for less than one year.

median age of 30. However, the median ages for the social workers were in the reverse order—32 when they received their M.S.W. degrees and 23 when drinking first interfered. These particular social workers went to graduate school later than is customary for reasons noted below, but we have no ready explanation for their report of interference seven years earlier than the other groups. Of the 34 college women who had graduated, three-quarters (74%) obtained their bachelor's degree in their early twenties (age 20 to 24), and the median age when drinking began to interfere with their lives was 27.

Thus, five of the six groups obtained their professional degrees or completed their basic professional training at least four years on the average before the onset of alcoholism, as we have defined it. The findings for the social workers are atypical because of the large proportion (44%) who obtained their master's degree after they had recovered from alcoholism. Many had been interested in making a career of counseling other alcoholics, saw the advantages of earning a degree, and chose social work as the most practical professional training for their purpose; their drinking experience therefore entirely antedated the start of their professional training.

What is the class standing in professional school of alcoholics in high-status occupations? As shown in Table 3.3, almost two-thirds (64%) of the 322 subjects who gave this information were clustered in the top third of their graduating classes, while only 6 percent were in the lowest third. Most of those not reporting this item claimed that their professional schools did not provide these rankings, which we verified in a partial check with some schools. The proportions in the top third ranged from 54 percent of the physicians to 73 percent of the social workers. Thus, these subjects claim that they were academic high achievers. Whether or not they were *overachievers* is impossible to say since we had no way to determine their actual ability. Perhaps these were people working at capacity in an attempt to win reassurance in the currency of the academic realm—that is, good grades. Perhaps they were among the most talented to begin with.

As Lincoln long ago suggested, "The demon of intemperance ever seems to have delighted in sucking the blood of genius . . . , more promising in youth than all his fellows . . . ; he seems ever to have gone forth like the Egyptian angel of death,

Table 3.3 Class Standing in Professional School According to Profession

| Class Standing | All Subjects Reporting Standing[b] $N =$ (322) | Profession[a] | | | | |
		Physicians (82)	Dentists (48)	Nurses (89)	Attorneys (55)	Social Workers (48)
Top third	64%	54%	65%	66%	67%	73%
Middle third	30	40	33	28	20	25
Lowest third	6	6	2	6	13	2
	100%	100%	100%	100%	100%	100%

[a]Excluding the college women group.
[b]Class standing in professional school was not provided to most of those 29 subjects (8%) who did not report this information.

commissioned to slay, if not the first, the fairest of every family" (13).

Perhaps our subjects are merely atypical in that they represent a group able to recognize and identify an alcoholism problem, able to find their way to A.A., and then use it successfully to remain sober for at least a year. They are the survivors and we know nothing of the others who continued to drink and to deny their problem.

Perhaps they simply had to impress us or didn't remember accurately, but interviewers commented repeatedly that this question seemed to be important to the respondents who offered detailed information and spoke with great pride of this often long-past achievement. The nurses from diploma schools who reported being in classes so small that class standing had little importance would then recite "exact" examination scores. Physicians, dentists, and lawyers often gave prompt responses, such as "I was number eight in a class of sixty-seven." If this was a lie, it was one that had been well practiced and was offered without hesitation.

If it is true that good grades and alcoholism go together in professional school, and perhaps in college as well, then this may be one of the very few early identifiable risk factors. It would pose a dilemma for those zealots who hope to prevent alcoholism in the professions by screening for it prior to admission, since perhaps that might mean screening out the most talented, as well as the most problematic. Either way, this particular finding could and should be verified.

Respondents attended their first A.A. meeting at a median age of 40, about 11 years after drinking started to interfere (Table 3.1). They had their last drink 2 years after that at a median age of 42. Thus, the alcoholics in our study, who typically started getting drunk regularly at 26, had their last drink an average of 16 years later.

It has been theorized that the course of alcoholism is shorter for women and for persons who are also addicted to other drugs; that is, being female or having other addictions might have a telescoping effect on the interval between the onset of regular drinking and getting into serious trouble because of it (14,15,16). Women in our study started drinking regularly at a median age of 21, two years later than did men (Table 3.1). On the other hand, women reported that drinking started to interfere with their lives at a median age of 28, two years earlier than the men. Thus, there did seem to be a telescoping of the drinking history among the women in our study, who started having serious trouble from drinking only 7 years after beginning to drink regularly, compared to 11 years for the men. However, the telescoping effect for those addicted to other drugs did not seem to be as large as the effect of being female (Table 3.1).

The telescoping of alcoholism symptoms for women is also demonstrated by their having a shorter period of active alcoholism compared to men. The duration of active alcoholism is considered the interval from the time when drinking first interfered with the subject's life to the very last drink. Forty-one percent of the women but only 29 percent of the men reported less than eight years of active alcoholism.

Almost two-fifths of both the men and the women had received psychiatric treatment for their alcoholism before achieving sobriety in A.A. However, a larger proportion of the men had been institutionalized at least once for alcoholism, although their first admission occurred at an older median age than the women (men, 68 percent and 39 years; women, 58 percent and 34 years).

The men first became concerned about their own drinking when slightly older than the women, although there was no gender difference in the age when another person first expressed concern. Perhaps because of differences in marital status, the concerned person for the men was most often a family member, while the concerned person for the women was equally likely to be a friend or other nonrelative. There were some sex differences in factors precipitating A.A. contact: men more often mentioned family pressures, economic pressures, and professional difficulties; women were more likely to cite health problems, remorse, guilt, or shame.

ADDICTION TO OTHER DRUGS

Ascertaining and evaluating the use of drugs other than alcohol in our study was more difficult. While A.A. discourages the use of any mood-changing drugs that can cause addiction (other than the ubiquitous use of tobacco and caffeine), its only requirement for membership is a desire to stop drinking. Some of our subjects were still using drugs. Some might not admit it at all and others might minimize it. Denial of current problems is common in alcoholics who continue to drink as well as among users of legally available drugs since to admit to a current problem invites the discomfort of self-examination and risks questions and criticism from others. We decided to ask whether a given drug had been used at all other than as an inpatient in a hospital or similar setting where someone else was controlling its administration. We also asked whether it was self-prescribed or on prescription, whether it was taken orally or by self-injection, whether this preceded or followed the last drink (or both), and finally whether the person was or had been addicted to it. If there was a clear statement that, yes, there was addiction, we accepted it. We did not define the word "addiction" for the respondent. If there appeared to be indecision and qualification of the answer, the person was considered as not having been addicted.

We also had to decide whether to regard dependence on mild narcotics in the same way as dependence on "hard" drugs. Was reported addiction to oral Percodan or terpin hydrate with codeine to be classed with the self-injection of Demerol? We decided to group Talwin (technically not a narcotic) with Demerol and morphine as "hard narcotics" and to regard Percodan and codeine as "soft narcotics." Overall, 45 subjects reported previous addiction to narcotics in the first interview; 33 of them were addicted to "hard" narcotics, including 16 also with a "soft" narcotic addiction. Only 12 reported addiction to "soft" but not to "hard" narcotics, and 9 were also addicted to one or more nonnarcotic drugs. No one mentioned addiction to Darvon who was not already included in one of the other "addiction groups" as well, nor did anyone at initial interview report Talwin addiction who had not also experienced addiction to another "hard" narcotic.

Physicians and nurses, as expected, were the professionals most likely to report addiction to "hard" narcotics. Addiction to these drugs was reported by 14 and 12 percent of the physicians and nurses, respectively (Table 3.4). The 197 respondents in these two professions, comprising just under one-half (48%) of the sample, accounted for four-fifths (79%) of the professionals reporting hard narcotic addiction. None of the attorneys and only 1 dentist did so, along with 4 of the social workers and 2 college women.

Table 3.4 Addiction Status According to Profession and Sex

		Profession						Sex	
Addiction Status	All Subjects N = (407)	Physicians (97)	Dentists (49)	Nurses (100)	Attorneys (55)	Social Workers (50)	College Women (56)	Men (214)	Women (193)
Alcohol only	64%	57%	65%	62%	73%	68%	64%	63%	65%
Alcohol plus:									
Nonnarcotic drugs[a]	25	25	33	23	23	22	28	26	25
"Soft" narcotics[a]	3	4	—	3	4	2	4	3	2
"Hard" narcotics[b]	8	14	2	12	—	8	4	8	8
Alcohol and other drugs[c]	(36%)	(43%)	(35%)	(38%)	(27%)	(32%)	(36%)	(37%)	(35%)
	100%	100%	100%	100%	100%	100%	100%	100%	100%

[a] Including some subjects reporting addiction to nonnarcotics.
[b] Including some subjects reporting addiction to nonnarcotics or "soft" narcotics.
[c] Subjects reporting addiction to nonnarcotics, "soft" narcotics, or "hard" narcotics.

Physicians and nurses handle meperidine (Demerol ®) almost daily or have it close at hand for emergencies. All initially obtained their drugs through professional channels rather than on the street. Legal access alone may not be as significant as when this is combined with familiarity and easy physical access as well. Dentists ordinarily do not keep narcotics in the office, nor do they routinely prescribe drugs stronger than codeine for outpatients. Narcotics were obtained by the social workers and college women through the illicit networks that provide drugs to the population at large. In the case of one male social worker with a history of criminal activity, incarceration, and heavy use of injectable narcotics, social work training followed his recovery.

None of the 33 who reported hard narcotic addiction were being maintained on methadone. Several scoffed at the notion that prolonged use of opiates altered brain chemistry in such a way as to require their lifelong use. They had for long periods used large quantities of narcotics that were stronger and less adulterated than street drugs and had often developed a high degree of physical tolerance. Nonetheless, most insisted they were comfortable without drugs of any kind and, in some cases, had been so for many years. They were quite convincing. However, it is doubtful, given the attitude of most A.A. members, that the methadone-maintained addict, even if alcoholic by history and abstinent as well, would be very comfortable in their midst and it may be that such individuals are to be found elsewhere.

Frequently mentioned as a major difference between alcoholic men and women is the supposedly greater use of tranquilizers, sedatives, and "diet pills" by women (17). The reasons cited are that women have more contacts with physicians than men, are more often diagnosed as emotionally ill, are more willing to accept this diagnosis, and thus are more likely to be given psychotropic drugs (15). If this were true, one would indeed expect alcoholic women as well to have higher rates of other drug addiction than alcoholic men. In our study this was not borne out, at least not when reported in terms of "addiction" and when all the men were compared with all the women and variation among professions was ignored.

More than one-third (36%) of all subjects reported being addicted to drugs other than alcohol before the first interview, ranging from only 27 percent of the largely male attorneys to

43 percent of the all-male physician group (Table 3.4). One-quarter of all subjects reported being addicted to nonnarcotic drugs only. Among the medical professions, only the dentists followed this addiction pattern. Most of those who reported being addicted to hard or soft narcotics (11% of the total sample) stated that they had been addicted to other mood-altering drugs as well (87%). While access certainly influenced the category of drugs complicating the alcoholism, secondary addictions per se were almost the same for men and women—both overall and according to drug category (nonnarcotics and soft or hard narcotics).

USE OF DRUGS OTHER THAN ALCOHOL

When we studied drug use alone and not "addiction," 84 percent of all subjects and more women (91%) than men (79%) reported having used a variety of mood-altering drugs. ("Use" did not include drugs administered during an inpatient stay in a hospital or other institution, but did include the taking of any mood-altering drugs, legally or illegally obtained, anywhere other than an inpatient setting, no matter how brief or limited.) A somewhat larger proportion of medical professionals (20%) and men (19%), compared to nonmedical professionals (11%) and women (14%), were at least occasionally using some form of mood-changing drug at the time of the initial interview, though only two or three betrayed any concern about this, and interviewers were careful not to express any approval or disapproval. This included any use of a mood-altering drug whatsoever, even as minor as a single tranquilizer twice a year before air travel.

The vast majority of the respondents thus had at least some out-of-hospital exposure to mood-altering drugs other than alcohol in situations where the decision to take them was presumably to some extent their own. Use of these other drugs did not inevitably lead to addiction, but if we omit those who say they were never even exposed, the overall percent addicted to other drugs increases and men then report addiction more often than women. The proportion of all *users*, male users, and female users addicted to other drugs are 43, 48, and 39 percent, respectively.

The first professionals to be questioned, 146 male physicians and dentists, were asked in the initial interview about their use of 11 specific mood-altering drugs, including codeine and other narcotics. Unlisted tranquilizers and other mood-changing drugs that had been used were to be named by the respondents. Three additional drugs known to be increasingly used—Librium, Valium, and Placidyl—were added to the drugs listed by name in the nurses' questionnaire. The nonmedical professionals (attorneys, social workers, and college women) were asked about their use of 7 additional drugs, for a total of 21 specific mood-altering drugs. The identical list of 21 drugs, with unspecified ones to be named by the respondents, appeared in the follow-up schedules for all professions. It was not uncommon during the interview to find that the use of a category of drug was denied only to be readily acknowledged as soon as a particular drug within that category was mentioned by name.

Overall, barbiturates and amphetamines were the drugs that had been most commonly used by the respondents (48% and 44%, respectively), followed by meprobamate and codeine, which were taken by one-third of the total sample at least occasionally before the first interview. Of the drugs not specifically named in the physicians' and dentists' questionnaire, Librium and Valium were reported most often by the other subjects (48% and 24%, respectively).

It would be a mistake to conclude that the benzodiazepine drugs are of minor concern. These drugs simply were not available or were not yet widely used when most of our subjects stopped drinking and taking drugs. They appeared with increasing frequency in the later interviews, and we certainly see them in widespread use by physicians and nurses coming to treatment today. (One of the authors has been personally involved in the treatment of two physicians whose use of diazepam is noteworthy. One, a white male in his early thirties, had been injecting 80 mg/day intravenously plus swallowing additional tablets from time to time as he felt the need. Another, an older woman, had injected the same drug into her leg muscles and as a result developed considerable fibrosis and oozing around the injection sites. She came to treatment because of the resultant decline of her hemoglobin to six!) That choice of drug depends on availability and other considerations is self-evident. Whether there is more use of drugs by professionals now rather than simply a difference in the specific drug chosen for this use is beyond the scope of this study. Among the 11 drugs that appeared in all of the initial schedules, the reported use of bromides, barbiturates, chloral hydrate, and narcotics was very similar between the sexes. However, about 10 percent more women than men reported using amphetamines, other mood elevators, meprobamate, and phenothiazines, possibly reflecting a greater concern for weight control and the greater frequency with which women, rightly or wrongly, are diagnosed as being in a depressed or anxious state.

Although we asked very few questions about why alcohol and drugs were used, many respondents volunteered much the same story. They had not been taught as part of their professional education that alcohol leads to insomnia nor that it also contributes to agitation and depression. When these problems appeared after drinking, they were attributed to a host of other factors such as stress, fatigue, financial or marital concerns, or an underlying emotional problem. Help when sought was often from a friend, colleague, or therapist equally unaware of alcohol's causative role. Medication was then used in order to sleep or feel less tense but, in many cases, tolerance developed and increasing doses were needed. Amphetamines were used to combat fatigue and sometimes to alleviate the grogginess caused by sedatives, especially when there was need to drive a car, stay awake to prepare a brief, deliver a baby, work an extra shift, meet an emergency, or carry out some other demanding task.

Physicians and nurses in particular reported that they were reluctant to work "drugged" and felt that they obviously could not work with shaking hands or smelling of alcohol, so they decided to try a narcotic to see if that would help them work. For many it did. (Demerol was overwhelmingly the narcotic of choice, both because of its wide availability and its tendency to cause less pupillary constriction than other opiates.) Winick noted in 1974 that 2 percent of drug-dependent nurses and eight times as many (17%) drug-dependent physicians cited alcohol as a reason for starting drug use (2). Narcotics were often used sparingly over many months, with the user returning regularly to alcohol and other sedative hypnotics as the drugs of choice before a narcotic became a problem in its own right.

Although one may be aware of one's own slurred speech and motor incoordination while drinking, there is usually little conscious awareness of impaired cognition or judgment. Sedatives other than alcohol reportedly were more likely to make the user feel dull and slowed down, hence the seemingly contradictory statement that narcotics were used in an attempt to avoid working while drugged.

SEQUENCE OF DRUG USE

Respondents were asked about the order in which they first had used alcohol, nonnarcotics, codeine, and "hard" narcotics. This question series, unfortunately, appeared in the follow-up but not in the first interview, so that responses are available only for the 362 subjects (89%) who were interviewed a second time. Nine-tenths reported that alcohol was the first mood-altering drug they had used, including 12 percent who had never used any of the other drugs. Most of those who had not used alcohol first had been given prescribed medication during childhood. As before, more women than men indicated that they had sometimes used drugs other than alcohol (the same as in the first interview; 91% of women and 79% of men, in the reinterview). Almost nine-tenths (86%) reported that they had used nonnarcotics; codeine and "hard" narcotic use was reported by 44 percent and 16 percent, respectively.

For those who had used these other drugs, the sequence most often was alcohol first, then nonnarcotics, and finally "hard" narcotics or codeine. However, about one-quarter of the subjects addicted to narcotics reported that they had started using more than one of these drug categories in the same year. Moreover, a few indicated taking whatever pills were available and occasionally being unable to remember what it was that they had taken. (One man said simply, "If, when it came in the mail, it said 'warning—may be habit forming,' I swallowed it.")

SMOKING

Those of us who sometimes design residential treatment programs usually reach a consensus easily about the need for alcoholics to avoid other mood-changing drugs of addiction. When no longer needed to prevent withdrawal problems, these drugs are discontinued promptly so that the common but temporary discomforts of mood swings, rebound anxiety, and insomnia can be managed in a controlled environment with support and understanding. Much more hotly debated are questions of whether to discourage the use of tobacco and caffeine.

There are zealots on both sides of these debates. While there seem to be no formal studies available, it appears that most of the treatment facilities simply make available only decaffeinated coffee during afternoons and evenings and restrict smoking only in certain areas or particular activities (not allowing it during group therapy, for example). Otherwise patients are left alone to decide these matters. To give up alcohol and the other mood-changing drugs is considered challenge enough for the moment, particularly during the turbulent early sobriety period. There are enough power struggles inherent in breaking down denial and attempting to win a firm commitment to the need for abstinence without inviting additional battles, be they internal or between patient and staff, many of whom are themselves smokers.

Since alcoholics and heavy drinkers commonly are heavy smokers as well, we wondered whether our subjects stopped smoking as they grew older and as the years of sobriety and ability to tolerate stress without drinking increased. We were interested as well in whether those in health care would be more likely to have done so than the others. We thought that doctors and nurses would stop smoking more frequently than attorneys and the other educated women because they were exposed to better information about smoking, witnessed its effects on patients, and were probably also aware of their own influence as role models. Since our social workers were not based in hospitals, we report them here as not in a health-care profession. Questions about smoking were only asked during the follow-up interviews. Since only a handful had stopped smoking before or simultaneously with stopping drinking, these are included in Table 3.5. Two-fifths (41%) of the 320 previous smokers had stopped. However, at least for the present sample, the medical professionals were actually less likely to stop smoking than the others.

The pattern then is that alcohol is the first drug used on a regular basis. Since most subjects report the onset of regular drinking to drunkenness and interference with their lives at much the same age, whether or not this occurs during graduate school is largely a function of the timing and length of the training itself.

Table 3.5   Smoking at Follow-up According to Profession and Sex

	All Subjects N = (362)	Profession[a]		Sex	
		Medical (219)	Other (143)	Men (191)	Women (171)
Continued smoking[b]	52%	58%	43%	52%	52%
Stopped smoking	36	31	45	38	35
Never smoked	12	11	12	10	13
	100%	100%	100%	100%	100%

[a] "Medical" professions include physicians, dentists, and nurses; "Other" professions include attorneys, social workers, and college women.
[b] Including four physicians, five attorneys, and one social worker who switched from cigarettes to pipes.

For physicians, dentists, attorneys, and probably for other professions requiring four years or more of education after college, heavy drinking is usually present before the degree is in hand. Alcoholism for them appears relatively soon after graduation. For nurses and those whose training need not extend more than three years beyond high school to gain a license, graduation occurs earlier, the student is several years younger, and the warning signs of alcoholism are not yet as likely to be apparent to student or faculty.

By regarding alcoholism as a disease with fairly predictable milestones, we can spare ourselves the attempt to explain its timing as a function of life circumstances. Young physicians and attorneys are not then seen as drinking because of the change in status from student to practitioner but simply as people who suffer from a disorder more likely to be manifest at age 30 than 20. We are also spared the attempt to explain drinking among nurses after many more years of actual work experience in terms of career "burnout."

If we know the ages at which benchmarks in alcoholism usually are passed and the ages during which professional training occurs, it becomes easier to plan screening procedures as well as educational or intervention efforts. For those at the doctoral level in all fields, graduate education usually comes well after basic life-style and drinking patterns have been established. For those going directly from high school into professional training, there may still be time to influence drinking behavior.

RISK FACTORS

George Vaillant has elegantly summarized the various etiological theories of alcoholism and how they reflect the many attempts to predict its occurrence (9). He concludes that there are three areas in which alcoholics appear to be premorbidly different from asymptomatic drinkers. First, alcoholics are more likely to come from ethnic groups that tolerate adult drunkenness while discouraging children and adolescents from learning safe drinking practices, such as consumption of low-proof alcoholic beverages at ceremonies and with meals. Second, future alcoholics are much more likely to have other alcoholics in the immediate family. (That there is a clear genetic component to alcoholism has now been demonstrated beyond a reasonable doubt, and the nature versus nurture controversy for both male and female alcoholism has subsided.) Third, thus far demonstrated for men only, in the absence of similar studies for women, is a history of antisocial behavior in adolescence.

Personality and Ethnicity

We made no attempt to assess premorbid personality patterns in our subjects. Since most professional schools attempt to evaluate character and personality as well as academic ability, the more obvious sociopaths probably fail to gain admission. The protection afforded by membership in a Jewish or Mediterranean ethnic group, however, may well be partially overcome as an individual is successful enough to become integrated into society and to have completed professional training. Adapting to a new culture brings both benefits and risks, and peer pressure is close at the heels of parental behavior in determining attitudes about both other drugs and alcohol.

Alcoholic Parents

Parental alcoholism may be of special interest to members of the helping professions. In the past decade there has been an enormous surge of interest in the effect of family alcoholism on children and, in particular, its residual effect on the adult children of alcoholics. Black (18) and others (17,19,20) have described several different response patterns to the chronic crisis of living in an alcoholic home. A much cited vignette is that of the family hero or heroine, often the oldest child, who takes on two roles—that of caretaker (as one parent fails in family responsibility while the other parent frequently becomes so caught up in the drinking that both are neglectful) and that of high achiever whose mission it is to demonstrate that the family really is alright (since otherwise this child could not perform so well).

If these particular children are the high achievers and the caretakers, what is more plausible than that they might also go on to become caretakers and managers in their choice of careers? Thomas Perrin, who conducts workshops for adult children of alcoholics, reports that he finds a disproportionately large number of nurses in his groups (21). While this is speculative, a high academic achievement pattern, as previously noted, is present in all of our professional groups, at least according to class standing at the time of graduation from professional school.

In any event, we asked about parental alcoholism and examined the answers for differences among professions. Of the entire sample, 35 percent had at least one alcoholic parent, a result consistent with the threefold increase in alcoholism in men reported by Vaillant and others (9). An unexpected and unexplained finding is a marked difference between men and women, with 29 percent of the men having an alcoholic parent as opposed to 41 percent of the women. Physicians, attorneys, and dentists were similar in this regard with 29, 27, and 24 percent, respectively. Somewhat more nurses than college women and social workers reported alcoholic parents (46%, 39%, and 38%, respectively).

Siblings and Children

Equal numbers of men and women reported alcoholic siblings (29% and 31%, respectively) at the initial interview and 10 percent of the men and 6 percent of the women reported having a child who was alcoholic. At follow-up this had risen to 12 percent of the men and 14 percent of the women. Time has been too short and many children are still too young for conclusions to be drawn about how many of them will ultimately be affected. Nevertheless, at follow-up 18 of the 47 men and women with known alcoholic children reported that at least one child was already in A.A. It is also far too early to predict whether parents' A.A. membership or recovery will decrease the risk for their children. In many cases the children were already in late adolescence or were even adults before the parental drinking stopped.

Response to Family Alcoholism

One common response to parental alcoholism is abstinence, but we have often heard alcoholics describe that, while their early dismay at the drinking led them to resolve never to drink, this decision obviously did not hold. What often *did* happen was that for a while they would stick to their resolve and indeed postpone the first drinking experience for months or even years. Vaillant notes that family alcoholism does not correlate with early onset of "alcohol abuse," and that, if anything, the opposite is true. If one might generalize from a collection of anecdotes, it may be that early caution does lead to a delay in experimentation, but that once a person has tried alcohol and finds it good and seemingly harmless as well, the decision is renegotiated and becomes instead a resolve to stop drinking should it ever become a problem.

We heard this so often, most frequently from men, that we wondered if onset of drinking and parental alcoholism were associated. (Note that we are talking about drinking, not about "abuse" or problem drinking.) If they were associated, would the sex of the alcoholic parent make a difference? Would a son, for instance, decide not to imitate an alcoholic father while seeing a mother as very different from himself and hence not such a powerful role model to be avoided? Since there is less alcoholism among women than among men even today, and there was considerably less when our subjects were children, there are fewer available alcoholic mothers.

Of our subjects, a total of 120 had alcoholic fathers as opposed to 48 with alcoholic mothers. Twenty-six reported that both parents were alcoholic. We found that of the 45 men with only alcoholic fathers, 20 was the median age when they started to drink regularly. If only the mother was alcoholic, the age was 18. For women, the ages were 19 and 17, respectively. Since the median age at which men *without* alcoholic fathers started drinking is 19, the sons of alcoholic fathers (though not those of alcoholic mothers) did show a slight delay by waiting until age

20, while the women, if anything, actually began drinking sooner. The other women in the sample, neither of whose parents were alcoholic, did not start drinking until age 21.

Profession as a Risk Factor

The question arises as to whether or not a given occupation or particular area within that occupation can itself be regarded as increasing risk for an individual. To be sure, access to alcohol and other drugs is necessary before one can use them destructively. It is also true that certain groups such as publicans in England and brewery workers in America exhibit a high prevalence of alcoholism. Nurses working on surgical floors, in anesthesia, and in coronary care units are said to be particularly prone to use Demerol; nurses doing private duty or night work in nursing homes reportedly are often alcoholic or addicted to other drugs. Actually, we need answers to two questions here. The first would be to see if these assertions are true. The second would be to explain why. Was there something in the setting that led to a chemical dependency, or did the individual consciously or otherwise seek out the setting in order to be able to drink or to use particular drugs?

Certain specialties within medicine have been reported to show a disproportionately higher rate of suicide. Suicidal behavior, in turn, is associated with the use of drugs and alcohol (22). Other studies have failed to confirm this initial impression, and a pooling of studies of alcoholic physicians in treatment reported by a variety of hospitals makes it appear that the seeming differences in specialties are artifacts that result from small sample size or referral patterns to a given facility. It is our impression that the group at highest risk of developing alcoholism among medical professionals is made up of individuals who, while ostensibly themselves free of other drug and alcohol problems, chose to make a career of researching or treating these problems in others. Marty Mann, founder of the National Council on Alcoholism, once said (23), "It really looks like it's a contagious disease." It does.

Certainly, people who fear observation but need access to drugs will arrange to work at times and places that meet their needs. To learn the rest, we will need to learn more about when and how career choices are made, and how these choices relate to drinking and drug use at the time. Ideally, these should be prospective studies, but it would have been useful to ask our subjects what they could remember about how these decisions were made.

REFERENCES

1. R. E. Wright-Sinclair, "Cause of Death in Colonial Doctors," *New Zealand Medical Journal 88*: 1978, pp. 49–51.

2. C. Winick, "Drug Dependence among Nurses," in: *Sociological Aspects of Drug Dependence*, C. Winick, ed., Cleveland: CRC Press, 1974, pp. 155–65.

3. W. D. Partlow, "Alcoholism and Drug Addiction among Physicians in Alabama," *Transactions of Medical Association of Alabama*, 1914, pp. 685–91.

4. National Institute on Alcohol Abuse and Alcoholism, *Fourth Special Report to the U.S. Congress on Alcohol and Health*, Washington, D.C.: Department of Health and Human Services, 1981.

5. D. W. Goodwin, "Alcoholism and Heredity," *Journal of the National Association of Private Psychiatric Hospitals 12*: 1981, pp. 94–96.

6. M. Bohman et al., "Maternal Inheritance of Alcohol Abuse: Cross-Fostering Analysis of Adopted Women," *Archives of General Psychiatry 38*: 1981, pp. 963–69.

7. R. Cloninger et al., "Inheritance of Alcohol Abuse: Cross-Fostering Analysis of Adopted Men," *Archives of General Psychiatry 38*: 1981, pp. 861–68.

8. R. Elmasian et al., "Event-Related Brain Potentials Are Different in Individuals at High Risk and Low Risk for Developing Alcoholism," *Proceedings of the National Academy of Science 79*: December 1982, pp. 7900–3.

9. G. E. Vaillant, *The Natural History of Alcoholism*, Cambridge, Mass.: Harvard University Press, 1983.

10. P. G. Marden, "Prevalence of Alcohol Abuse in the Gay Population in the United States," prepared for the National Institute of Alcohol Abuse and Alcoholism, Rockville, Md., January 1980.

11. M. Keller, "Definition of Alcoholism," *Quarterly Journal of Studies on Alcohol 21*: 1960, pp. 125–34.

12. M. B. Bailey et al., *Alcoholics Anonymous: Pathway to Recovery*, New York: National Council on Alcoholism, 1965.

13. A. Lincoln, Address to Washington Temperance Society, Springfield, Ill.: February 22, 1842.

14. M. J. Ashley et al., "Morbidity in Alcoholics: Evidence for Accelerated Development of Physical Disease in Women," *Archives of Internal Medicine 137*: 1977, pp. 883-87.

15. E. S. Gomberg, "Alcoholism and Women: State of Knowledge Today," in: *Alcohol Abuse among Women: Special Problems and Unmet Needs*, Washington, D.C.: U.S. Government Printing Office, from U.S. Senate Subcommittee on Alcoholism and Narcotics, Committee on Labor and Public Welfare Hearing, September 29, 1976, pp. 228-40.

16. J. Curlee, "A Comparison of Male and Female Patients at an Alcoholism Treatment Center," *Journal of Psychology 74*: 1970, pp. 239-47.

17. E. M. Corrigan, *Alcoholic Women in Treatment*, New York: Oxford University Press, 1980.

18. C. Black, *It Will Never Happen to Me*, Denver: MAC, 1982.

19. C. Deutsch, *Broken Bottles, Broken Dreams*, New York: Teachers College Press, 1982.

20. M. Woodside, *Children of Alcoholics*, Report to H. L. Carey, Governor, State of New York, Albany: Division of Alcoholism and Alcohol Abuse, 1982.

21. T. Perrin, "Editorial," *COA Review*, July/August, 1983, p. 2.

22. P. H. Blachly et al., "Suicide by Physicians," *Bulletin of Suicidology*, December 1968, pp. 1-18.

23. M. Mann, Personal Communication, 1979.

4

Consequences and Sanctions

Alcoholism in its early stages can be easily concealed in our culture. We are permissive about heavy drinking and ambivalent about the degree to which even frank drunkenness is accepted. Signs of beginning trouble may be explained away as isolated events—for instance, the results of a wedding, promotion, holiday, tragedy, unusual fatigue, or an unwise mixing of drinks. If the reason is plausible, we conclude with relief that a friend or colleague is not really in trouble.

Members of the immediate household are usually the first to become aware of a drinking problem and first to broach the subject. Close friends may also see that all is not well, but usually their early, tentative words of caution are dismissed or rationalized away. Many of our subjects said that, as friends began to criticize, if a choice had to be made between continued heavy drinking and their approval, it was the friends that had to go. Their expression of concern was remembered with gratitude some years later, but at the time they were replaced by more heavy drinkers in whose presence the alcoholic felt less self-conscious. Subsequent statements such as, "I don't drink any more than anyone else we know," may reflect the truth but do not acknowledge that a new circle of friends has been chosen for that very reason.

Even though denial of a drinking problem is typical of both the alcoholic and the loyal family member, its concealment eventually becomes more difficult as matters get worse. Signs of trouble become visible to others. There are few secrets in small towns and even in large cities a professional community often has a highly developed grapevine. How then did peers and the community at large respond as the drinking problem of our subjects became increasingly apparent? Since a colleague's arrest, jailing, hospitalization, or overt suicide attempt is likely to be known and should alert members of the profession that something is amiss, we can ask how often these events occurred and the nature of both formal and informal responses to them.

OVERDOSES AND SUICIDE ATTEMPTS

Overt suicide attempts before the first interview were reported at that time by 17 percent of the men and 30 percent of the women, a total of 23 percent of the original 407 respondents. Other studies have shown women to be more likely to attempt suicide than men, and men more likely than women to complete a suicide successfully (1,2). College women and nurses were most likely to report having made at least one attempt (32% and 31%, respectively), followed in order by social workers, dentists, attorneys, and physicians (24%, 20%, 18%, and 14%, respectively). While it has been reported that physicians and dentists are more prone to suicide than other professional groups (3,4,5), data remain inconclusive except in the case of women physicians who, along with women chemists, do indeed appear to be at higher risk than women in other fields (6,7,8). It may well be that, since women make more attempts than men, those with medical or similar training are in more danger of succeeding, if only because they are more knowledgeable about effective methods. If this is the case, then nurses as well as women physicians should prove to be at greater risk of dying than nonmedical women (if they attempt suicide) and their rates should be higher—an unsettled question that deserves attention.

Overdoses taken during periods of heavy drinking and other drug use may or may not have been accidental. Not all overdoses were suicide attempts, nor was drug overdose the only suicide method used. Other events as well, such as driving a car into a tree, may have been deliberate, accidental, or the result of very mixed motivation. Details of these happenings were often lost in the haze of alcohol-induced or posttraumatic amnesia. When a subject was uncertain about whether a self-destructive event had been attempted suicide, we considered that it was not. If the subject claimed that it was, that was accepted as true. These are, of course, the retrospective reports of survivors and speculation about the unconscious remains. We can say nothing about those who were successful in taking their own lives, men and women whose methods and personalities may have been quite different.

At the initial interview we asked if there had ever been a serious sedative overdose and then if there had been overt suicide attempts. We did not at the time consider that a reply of "yes, one" to both questions would leave us ignorant as to whether the overdose represented the attempt or if these were two unrelated events. Accordingly, we devised a different question series, both to evaluate consistency of response from one interview to another and to learn more detail about the previous attempts.

Face-to-face reinterviews were obtained with 86 percent (350) of the 407 original subjects. (See Chapter 6.) This group included 76 (80 percent) of the original 95 attempters, representing 21 percent of all those reinterviewed. Of these, 55 percent had made a single attempt, 25 percent had made two, and 10 percent had made three or more attempts. A recent American Medical Association (AMA) pilot study on physician suicide has concentrated on unexplained deaths under the age of 40 (9) and, indeed, 73 percent of our attempters said that their first attempt did occur in that age range, but only 66 percent of the most recent attempts fell before age 40.

There was a clear and rather dramatic correlation between the use of other drugs and a history of attempted suicide, with only 16 percent of those reporting a history of addiction to alcohol alone versus 52 percent of the 33 people with a history of "hard" narcotic addiction reporting attempts. When addiction to any additional drug other than a "hard" narcotic occurs, the intermediate figure of 30 percent appears! An attempt to compare these findings with previous studies ended in frustration. While numerous authors have noted that alcoholic physicians also use other drugs, it is frequently impossible to tell if what is meant is occasional use or serious addiction. Even Blachly's excellent study of physician suicide, which points to the large numbers who drank heavily or were considered to have a problem with other drugs, does not make clear whether these were two separate populations—that is, drug users versus drinkers—overlapping populations, or essentially the same population in trouble with both alcohol and other drugs simultaneously (10). If indeed it is narcotic addiction that increases the prevalence of suicide attempts, then physicians and nurses, male or female, should have higher rates compared to others of similar social and educational backgrounds.

It is true that, in our study, attempts actually are described slightly more often by those not in health care than by those who are, but we must stress again that these are survivors. If physicians, nurses, and dentists are, as postulated above, more efficient at killing themselves than attorneys or women in other careers, fewer of them should remain alive to describe their failures. If it is also true that previous attempters are a high risk group, then this relative difference should hold within the confines of each occupational category.

We asked the 76 reinterviewed attempters about methods used, whether or not notes were left, if there had been efforts to make the suicide appear to be an accident, and who else had known about it.

By far the most common method was drug overdose, named by 43 of the 76 (57%). Seven had tried to disguise the attempt as an accident, three of them deliberately crashing an automobile. Fourteen had cut or stabbed themselves or had slashed wrists. One had used a poison. The rest used other methods. Only five had left notes and quite frequently the failed attempt was concealed. In over half of these attempts, no one else knew. (Family knew of about one-third of these attempts; others were only half as likely as family to know.)

While we did not specifically ask the reason for failure, one was often volunteered. Unawareness of the degree to which drug tolerance had developed was very common. One physician described hiding his car in a clump of trees, sitting down in a haystack, and injecting an enormous quantity of narcotic into a vein. He woke up again sometime later little the worse for the experience. (This man was determined to make us believe that this had been a serious attempt, not a gesture.) Others underestimated their ability to survive car crashes or leaps from high places. Serious fractures were sustained but they lived.

Most were under the influence of alcohol (58 of the 76) at the time an attempt was made, and virtually all were under the influence of some sort of drug, though only two were actively using "hard" narcotics that day. Barbiturates, tranquilizers, and other sedatives were commonly used. Three were using stimulants as well. Perhaps an additional reason for survival may simply be that drunkenness, whether the result of alcohol or of other sedatives, decreases one's efficiency in many areas, even that of self-destruction.

It is tempting to assume that suicidal people are those suffering primarily from affective disorders and even to account for their drinking on that basis. However, we heard repeatedly that the experience of active alcoholism itself had been intensely painful, that much of the misery seemed in retrospect to have been caused by the pervasive effects of the alcohol and drugs themselves, and that the suicide attempts were made in a state of confusion and poor judgment. Usually the person was drinking at the time, and alcohol itself was very much a part of the personal and professional upsets that were often present then. When the subject had been "clean and dry" for a period of time, most reported that suicidal ideation ceased altogether.

It has long been acknowledged that there are a great many suicides among alcoholics and a great many alcoholics among those who both attempt and complete suicide (1). Alcoholism has been variously seen as a form of chronic suicide (11) or even a suicide substitute, a way of "playing dead" (12). It has also been described, particularly for women, as a form of self-medication used to mask an underlying depression (13,14). If these formulations are true, then to stop drinking might well result in an increased number of more obvious acts of self-destruction. Indeed, Crawshaw and his colleagues in 1980 reported an epidemic of suicide among physicians on probation in Oregon, involving 6 of the 40 then under investigation (15). Of these 6, 5 used amphetamines or Demerol, 4 had alcohol problems, and all misused one or another of these. Fortunately, Shore continued to study the Oregon situation and reported that this pattern did not continue (16). It was a cluster of suicides that occurred in 1976 and 1977 and then ended.

If suicide in active alcoholism is seen not as yet another symptom of an underlying emotional problem but rather as a response to the pain and confusion of the drinking situation itself, then suicide rates in sober alcoholics should approximate those seen in the rest of the population. While the experiences of our subjects during the limited follow-up period would tend to support the second position, their numbers are small and we must repeat that we were studying the survivors—those who had been able to remain alive and sober and discoverable for interviewing in the first place.

LEGAL AND FORMAL SANCTIONS

Less than half of the subjects reported experiencing each of the professional and legal sanctions listed in Table 4.1. As expected, men were much more likely than women to have had trouble with the law, as reflected in the loss of a driver's license or being arrested or jailed because of their drinking. Men more often than women received admonishments from colleagues and warnings from an employer or professional society about their drinking. Except for the informal admonishments of colleagues, these professional and legal sanctions were experienced most often by those alcoholics also addicted to "hard" narcotics, and least often by those not addicted to any other additional drugs.

Many respondents volunteered that, while they had never actually been arrested or jailed because of their drinking, they easily could and probably should have been. Attorneys mentioned frequent commingling of client funds and stealing from trusts, rationalized initially as "borrowing." Undetected theft of drugs by medical professionals was common. Highway police were often prone to forgive violations when the driver was identified as a doctor, a judge, or an attorney, and women were often driven or sent home by taxi rather than booked. Nonetheless, one-half of the men and one-sixth of the women were arrested, and most of these were jailed (Table 4.1). Except for arrests directly related to the illegal diversion of narcotics, most arrests took place while the individual was actively drinking and involved not only the offense (usually "drunk and disorderly" or a moving vehicle violation) but also a refusal to be courteous to or cooperate with the arresting officer.

HOSPITAL ADMISSIONS

Hospitalizations for alcoholism and alcohol-related illness were very common. Regardless of the official diagnosis at the time, we considered an admission alcohol related if the respondent felt that

Table 4.1 Professional and Legal Sanctions According to Sex and Addiction

| Sanctions | All Subjects (407) | Sex | | Addictions[a] | | |
		Men (214)	Women (193)	Alcohol Only (259)	Alcohol and Nonnarcotics (115)	Alcohol and "Hard" Narcotics (33)
Colleague's admonishment about drinking	38%	49%	25%	35%	43%	36%
Professional society or employer warning about drinking	22	25	19	18	29	30
Lost driver's license	12	16	7	7	18	24
Arrested	34	49	16	29	40	51
Jailed	26	39	13	21	35	42

[a]The category Alcohol and Nonnarcotics *does not* include any subjects who reported addiction to "hard" narcotics, but *does* include nine subjects who *also* reported addiction to codeine and three who *only* reported addiction to codeine. The category Alcohol and "Hard" Narcotics includes subjects who *also* reported addiction to nonnarcotics or "soft" narcotics.

it would not have occurred in the absence of drinking. Admissions directly caused by someone else's drinking were not included.

Medical professionals reported an average of twice as many alcohol-related hospital admissions as the nonmedical groups (4.8 versus 2.3 per subject, respectively). All subjects combined had a total of over 1,500 alcohol-related admissions! (See Table 4.2.)

The physicians had the most admissions with an average of 6.3 separate hospitalizations and 4.7 months in hospitals. The nurses reported the next largest average number of admissions and were more likely than the physicians to have been admitted to psychiatric rather than medical settings. The attorneys on average had the fewest admissions and spent the least time as inpatients (1.9 admissions and less than four weeks in the hospital). There is no obvious reason for these rather dramatic differences. While most of those addicted to narcotics were the physicians and nurses, that alone fails to enlighten. Hospital employees are said by health insurance underwriters to make more heavy use of in-patient facilities than are other groups of workers, but no explanation is offered.

RESPONSE OF COLLEAGUES

It is hard to believe that the colleagues of the alcoholic were entirely unaware of what was happening, particularly since marital discord, divorce, and other signs of trouble were also common. Other sequelae of alcoholism such as regular morning drinking were reported by 60 percent of the sample, and drinking to relieve withdrawal symptoms was acknowledged by 76 percent (Table 4.3). About 62 percent reported drinking during working hours, with a range of 37 percent of the nurses doing so to 80 percent of the attorneys.

We asked whether there had been a comment by a colleague or superior, no matter how informal the admonition, that directly addressed the issue of excessive drinking rather than a secondary problem such as lateness or poor job performance. Certainly an informal comment was the most common sanction reported. Formal sanctions were understandably less common than casual remarks, but it is striking that throughout their entire drinking careers, more than three-quarters of the nurses, two-fifths of the physicians, and about two-thirds of those in the other professions

Table 4.2 Inpatient Experiences According to Profession

Alcohol and Other Drug Admissions Before Initial Interview N =	Physicians (97)	Dentists (49)	Nurses (100)	Attorneys (55)	Social Workers (50)	College Women (56)
			Profession			
Average number of admissions per subject	6.3	3.2	4.1	1.9	2.4	2.6
Total time (in average number of months) per subject in inpatient treatment	4.7	2.7	3.3	0.8	1.9	3.3
Total time (in average number of months) per admission in inpatient treatment	0.7	0.8	0.8	0.4	0.8	1.3

could not remember any colleague or superior ever saying anything critical to them about their drinking (Table 4.4).

At the onset of this study we expected to find that physicians and dentists, who often practice alone or with little supervision, would experience fewer sanctions, either formal or informal, than those who worked for others or within hierarchical systems. We also thought that all medical professionals would be sanctioned more frequently than those less directly responsible for the lives of others. Although an attorney can lose a client's entire estate or even his freedom, just as an inept social worker can cost a parent the custody of a child, public perception seems to be that medical people are the most dangerous. Our expectations were not borne out.

The nurses, who we predicted would be the least likely to escape sanctions, turned out to experience the fewest. A possible explanation offered by several nurses is that frequent job changes are common and acceptable in nursing and that nurses often leave jobs voluntarily when they become aware that an employer is getting suspicious. Professional societies or employers were very unlikely to have warned dentists, most of whom were in solo private practice. On the other hand, physicians, who had more invested in privileges and referral networks at a given hospital, and were more visible to other staff, could not as readily undertake a "geographical cure" or as easily escape the notice of their colleagues. Aside from nurses, those professionals who were more likely to work for others, as expected, were warned more often by their employers.

Several nurses told of a pattern of career changes as drinking and its related problems increased. They moved away from positions of high visibility into areas where there was less supervision and fewer co-workers who might observe them. Day shifts gave way to regular evening or night duty. Jobs with high pressure and great responsibility would be relinquished with an explanation that the needs of a husband or children required a change of job site or hours. The intensive care unit would be abandoned for the nursing home nearer the home; regular staff positions were left for private duty or registry work. If the move was voluntary, poor references were rarely given. With evident relief all around, the departure solved the immediate problem.

Table 4.3 Experiences Related to Alcoholism According to Sex and Addiction

| Experiences Related to Alcoholism | All Subjects | Sex | | Addictions[a] | | |
| | | Men | Women | Alcohol Only | Alcohol and Nonnarcotics | Alcohol and "Hard" Narcotics |
$N=$	(407)	(214)	(193)	(259)	(115)	(33)
Solitary drinking	94%	92%	96%	93%	97%	94%
Rationalizing drinking[b]	93	92	93	92	93	97
Sneaking drinks	92	95	89	92	92	94
Loss of control[b]	91	91	92	90	92	100
Preoccupation with alcohol	89	88	91	88	91	94
Blackouts	88	87	90	86	92	91
Guilt about drinking	88	93	83	87	89	100
Gulping drinks	87	91	83	84	92	97
Errors of judgment and reasoning[c]	86	85	86	83	89	94
Drinking for relief of withdrawal symptoms[c]	76	81	70	72	80	91

74

Alcohol for relief of insomina	71	68	75	65	78	94
Drinking during working hours	62	75	47	57	70	70
Periods of total abstinence[b]	62	68	55	64	58	58
Regular morning drinking[b]	60	65	53	55	68	67
Benders or binges[c]	58	68	47	54	64	70
Geographic escape[b]	44	43	47	36	59	61
Auditory hallucinations[c]	39	44	34	32	48	67
Visual hallucinations[c]	33	36	30	27	42	52
Seizures[c]	18	21	15	13	21	46
Fatty liver	17	18	17	17	17	18
GI bleeding	15	17	12	12	17	24
Liver cirrhosis	7	7	6	6	6	12
Pancreatitis	7	6	8	5	12	6

[a] The category Alcohol and Nonnarcotics *does not* include any subjects who reported addiction to "hard" narcotics, but *does* include nine subjects who *also* reported addiction to codeine and three who *only* reported addiction to codeine. The category Alcohol and "Hard" Narcotics includes subjects who *also* reported addiction to nonnarcotics or "soft" narcotics.
[b] Middle-stage symptoms in the drinking history of alcoholics (17).
[c] Late-stage symptoms in the drinking history of alcoholics (17).

Table 4.4 Professional Sanctions According to Profession

	Profession					
Sanctions N =	Physicians (97)	Dentists (49)	Nurses (100)	Attorneys (55)	Social Workers (50)	College Women (56)
Colleague's admonishment about drinking	59%	37%	23%	38%	30%	34%
Professional society or employer warning about drinking	23	4	2	36	40	43
Lost hospital privileges	22	6	—	—	—	—
Malpractice suits	7	8	0	—	—	—
Loss of professional license	7	0	3	—	—	—

Just over one-quarter of all subjects, men and women alike, had been through periods of unemployment other than when institutionalized, which they attributed directly to drinking. We asked them when they had begun and when they had ended the most prestigious job (in their estimation) that they had *ever* held before they stopped drinking. The women had both attained and ended these jobs earlier than the men, starting at a median age of 29 and ending at 34. The men started at a median age of 32 and ended at 44, probably indicative of their different number of years of professional training. The men stayed at this job for 12 years on average, compared to only 5 years for the women.

Two explanations are suggested by this gender gap in the length of time at the most prestigious job. First, the men in our study were in professions that demanded a higher investment in job stability than were the women. Establishing oneself in a law firm, attaining academic rank, or earning hospital privileges can require an investment of time and effort that will not be abandoned lightly. Nurses, on the other hand, have little in the way of career ladders available to them and frequently are poorly rewarded either financially or with increased status by remaining with the same employer. Not only is this common to women's jobs in general, but women also are less likely to be questioned if they choose to stop working for a time. The demands of child care or of being a homemaker easily explain a job change, while a man who deliberately opts for fewer hours or less responsibility will be regarded with greater suspicion. As previously stated, the nurses comprise many of the women who reported leaving jobs when they sensed that they were on the verge of being reprimanded for their behavior. When storm clouds gathered on the horizon, they decided to initiate action themselves rather than remain to face what might be an unpleasant confrontation.

The median annual earnings for the men were more than three times greater than those for the women. This large sex differential in annual earnings reflects the known difference between the better paying, predominantly male professions, such as medicine, dentistry, or law, and the poorer paying, predominantly female professions of nursing or social work.

Actual firings were for all subjects quite rare, and many never had to stop working. Jobs were frequently altered without being relinquished entirely, sometimes voluntarily, sometimes at the suggestion of colleagues. Both status and responsibility would be lessened in an attempt to reduce stress or avoid embarrassment. Many were effectively demoted by their peers with a variety of reasons offered as explanation and with drinking rarely mentioned. This phenomenon has been called "job shrinkage" in industry to describe a pattern of work performance in which minimum requirements are met and there are no grounds for terminating an employee; however, the promise of full creativity and accomplishment which might otherwise be expected in the years of highest productivity is never kept.

Both nurses and female social workers described their coprofessionals as almost too willing to accept excuses long past the point when patience should have run out. "We nurse and nurture each other far too long and then we lynch!" said one nurse. Supervisors were described as falling into the role of treaters of their own staff, often clinging stubbornly to that position for long periods, then at last responding to what seemed like betrayal or ingratitude with anger and at times vindictiveness. Almost alone among the professions, nurses who have diverted drugs are still arrested, handcuffed, and led away from the hospital in full sight of their colleagues. And although it is hard to lose a nursing license, it is even harder to get one restored after recovery is well established.

Narcotic addiction also caused nurses to choose work sites where Demerol was readily available, usually in anesthesia, coronary care, or surgery. Only very rarely did a nurse tell us of using drugs intended for a patient. In most cases drugs were charted as having been given to patients who were in fact sound asleep. Leaving patients to suffer while the nurse used their drugs was not often necessary since a clever nurse could easily supply both the patient and herself.

It might appear that the physicians were detected and disciplined rather frequently. Nearly one-quarter had been confronted by an employer or medical society, and a similar number (many of them the same individuals) had lost hospital privileges (Table 4.4). Unfortunately, this often did not occur until there had been a felony conviction that forced colleagues to take action. Dentists are much less likely than physicians to hold hospital privileges and therefore less likely to lose them.

Bar associations were also described as reluctant to intervene until an arrest had occurred or a complaint was initiated by someone, usually not a colleague, which could not be ignored. Social workers mentioned that criticism could sometimes be defused quite easily by saying that they were in psychotherapy, thus trading on a supervisor's reluctance to interfere with that process.

A domino effect was often described in which an entanglement with the law would lead to publicity, a conviction, or both. This, in turn, would involve the medical society or licensing board and result in the loss of credentials or hospital privileges. Since legal problems were more common among those who diverted drugs more strictly controlled than alcohol and tranquilizers, it is not surprising that formal sanctions were more commonly applied to the "hard" narcotic addicts. At the same time, these subjects reported no greater number of informal sanctions than the others.

Even the simple informal admonishment was absent for three-quarters of the women and half of the men (Table 4.1). In other words, an entire drinking career ran its course for almost two-thirds of the entire group studied without as much as a single direct comment about drinking from any colleague or superior that could be remembered! Unless we choose to believe that these events were conveniently forgotten, it appears that the most common response to active alcoholism in a colleague, unless it was discussed among others rather than with the drinker, was silence.

The subjects in this study were all well into recovery at the time of the first interview, and all but two, both nurses, had regained their licenses to practice. Only a handful had lost them in the first place—three nurses who had also been addicted to "hard" narcotics and seven physicians. Four dentists and seven physicians were also sued for malpractice, but not necessarily for alcohol-related actions. One plastic surgeon claimed to have been sued only once, much less than his nonalcoholic peers in this litigation-prone field. Almost all (and for most this is still the case) entered treatment with license intact and with a practice having continued up to or close to the time of admission. For this reason, one must be cautious in accepting a return to practice as evidence per se of good treatment outcome in a professional, since this measurement may indicate merely that things are not demonstrably worse than prior to treatment.

PHYSICAL DEPENDENCE AND TOXIC EFFECTS

In asking ourselves why there was relatively little professional response to the distress of alcoholic colleagues (even less formal response than was provided by the police), one might question whether these were really advanced cases. Perhaps, as highly educated and privileged people, our subjects had received help early enough that their problems never became severe. Dr. E. M. Jellinek has categorized alcoholism symptoms into early, middle, and late stages (17). As indicated in Table 4.3, most of our respondents reported experiences that are included among the signs of far advanced alcoholism.

About nine-tenths of all respondents reported such common alcoholism-related experiences as solitary drinking, rationalizing or guilt about drinking, loss of control, preoccupation with alcohol, blackouts, sneaking or gulping drinks, and errors of judgment related to drinking (Table 4.3). Men somewhat more often than women indicated that they had sneaked or gulped drinks and had feelings of guilt about their drinking, but there was little difference in the frequency of occurrence of many other experiences.

A somewhat smaller proportion of the subjects (58 to 76 percent) reported drinking for relief of withdrawal symptoms or insomnia, drinking during working hours, periods of total abstinence, drinking regularly in the morning, and binges or benders. Men were more likely to have had all of these alcoholism-related experiences, except for using alcohol to relieve insomnia. More men than women indicated drinking during working hours, probably both because a larger proportion of men continued working outside of the home throughout all or most of the years of active alcoholism and because of the long and irregular hours worked by many self-employed professionals. Still smaller proportions reported having experienced auditory or visual hallucinations and attempting geographic escape. Seizures and fatty liver had occurred in almost one-fifth of the cases, and 7 percent reported cirrhosis of the liver and pancreatitis. Alcohol-related liver disease was reported with the same frequency by both sexes, while men somewhat more often than women had seizures and gastrointestinal bleeding.

In general, the alcoholics addicted to prescription drugs were more likely to have had these experiences than those alcoholics without any other addictions, and those addicted to "hard" narcotics as well were the most likely to report these experiences. Among the experiences most highly correlated with other drug addictions were drinking for relief of withdrawal symptoms or insomnia, regular morning drinking, and seizures, all commonly related to physical dependency (although Demerol itself can induce seizures). Drinking for withdrawal or insomnia relief, guilt about drinking, gastrointestinal bleeding, and especially seizures, auditory and visual hallucinations, and liver cirrhosis were markedly associated with "hard" narcotics addiction.

Although Jellinek's work may be criticized, common sense suggests that, when most of the sample admit to loss of control when drinking and a large majority clearly indicate signs of physical dependency as well, these were not mild cases who could be expected to pass unnoticed by their peers. The reasons for the failure to intervene must be sought elsewhere. Whether lawyers, social workers, and health-care professionals as a group ignore the plight of their peers more than college professors, airline pilots, politicians, or clergy is for now a matter of conjecture.

The failure to act probably stemmed not from any single cause but rather from several. Some alcoholic men and women are remarkably clever at concealing their drinking, particularly at work. Their colleagues usually are prepared to recognize alcoholism only in its final stages and do not expect to find it in their peers. They are not sure what they are seeing, and the lack of certainty breeds hesitation. Nor do they wish to appear judgmental about another's private life and personal behavior. There is fear that, if approached, the drinker will respond with anger and denial, perhaps even with a threat of legal reprisal. If help is resisted, it may be awkward to go on working with the person.

Ignorance of what to say or how to say it compounds the difficulty. The one who blows the whistle often is treated as an alarmist by others who respond with excuses for the abnormal behavior rather than by volunteering to join in a confrontation. To do nothing and to pretend ignorance are actions that avoid criticism. Others seem equally reluctant to acknowledge or call attention to the situation. If, in addition, one knows little about available treatment or is aware only of disciplinary systems that have historically been slow to act and inept or merely punitive when at last they do, it is hard to see the value in confronting an alcoholic with the problem.

REFERENCES

1. D. W. Goodwin, "Alcoholism and Suicide: Association Factors," in: *Encyclopedic Handbook of Alcoholism*, E. M. Pattison and E. Kaufman, eds., New York: Gardner Press, 1982, pp. 655–62.

2. N. L. Farberow, "Crisis, Disaster and Suicide: Theory and Therapy," in: *Essays in Self-Destruction*, E. Schneidman, ed., New York: Science House, 1967, pp. 373–98.

3. P. H. Blachly et al., "Suicide in Professional Groups," *New England Journal of Medicine 268*: June 6, 1963, pp. 1278–82.

4. R. C. Steppacher and J. S. Mausner, "Suicide in Male and Female Physicians," *Journal of the American Medical Association 228*: April 15, 1974, pp. 323–28.

5. R. J. Shankle, "Suicide, Divorce and Alcoholism among Dentists: Fact or Myth?" *North Carolina Dental Journal 60*: 1977, pp. 12–15.

6. A. G. Craig and F. N. Pitts, "Suicide by Physicians," *Diseases of the Nervous System 29*: 1968, pp. 763–72.

7. F. P. Li, "Suicide among Chemists," *Archives of Environmental Health 19*: 1969, pp. 518–20.

8. J. S. Mausner and R. C. Steppacher, "Suicide in Professionals: A Study of Male and Female Psychologists," *American Journal of Epidemiology 98*: 1973, pp. 436–45.

9. Proceedings of the American Medical Association House of Delegates, Chicago, December 1982.

10. P. H. Blachly et al., "Suicide by Physicians," *Bulletin of Suicidology*, December 1968, pp. 1–18.

11. K. A. Menninger, *Man Against Himself*, New York: Harcourt, Brace, 1938.

12. E. G. Palola et al., "Alcoholism and Suicidal Behavior," in: *Society, Culture and Drinking Patterns*, D. J. Pittman and C. R. Snyder, eds., New York: Wiley, 1962, pp. 511–34.

13. J. R. Stevens and J. Shore, "Female Physicians and Primary Affective Disorder" (letter, including replies by F. N. Pitts and A. Welner), *Archives of General Psychiatry 37*: 1980, pp. 110–11.

14. M. A. Schuckit et al., "Alcoholism: I. Two Types of Alcoholism in Women," *Archives of General Psychiatry 20*: 1969, pp. 301–6.

15. R. Crawshaw et al., "An Epidemic of Suicide among Physicians on Probation," *Journal of the American Medical Association 243*: May 16, 1980, pp. 1915–17.

16. J. H. Shore, "The Impaired Physician: Four Years After Probation," *Journal of the American Medical Association 248*: December 17, 1982, pp. 3127–30.

17. J. E. Royce, *Alcohol Problems and Alcoholism*, New York: The Free Press, 1981.

5

Seeking Treatment

Whether or not the use of alcohol is identified as the root of the individual's increasing difficulties, many alcoholics continue to drink until they die. Death may result from suicide, from accidents, from illnesses like cirrhosis and pancreatitis, or from malignancies directly related to the toxic effects of alcohol itself. Even more often, alcoholics die from the same physical illnesses that kill everyone else. However, if the drinking continues, death does occur considerably earlier among alcoholics than nonalcoholics (1,2,3,4). Some heavy drinkers recognize that alcohol is causing trouble and are able to change drinking patterns successfully. Others make a "command decision" and stop drinking altogether without seeking outside assistance. We still lack adequate data to let us know how many in either the lay population or in the professions follow these routes. Probably most alcoholics and their families are forced eventually to admit that something is very wrong. When home remedies have failed, the alcoholics may be forced by others or by circumstances to seek help.

CLERGY

Where help is sought reflects the way in which a problem is conceptualized. If one sees alcoholism as basically a moral failing, a lack of willpower, or perhaps merely as self-indulgent behavior, it makes sense to turn to those who speak with authority

about ethical matters, often members of the clergy. Perhaps
through prayer or "taking the pledge" or through the words and
insight of an outsider, the drinker can be helped to see the harm
being done and persuaded to change behavior. (We still hear
members of the press refer to "reformed" alcoholics. There are no
similar references to "reformed" diabetics or "reformed" hypertensives, individuals whose illnesses have not carried the same
moral overtones as alcoholism.)

In the study by Bailey et al. (1965) in New York City, 1,058 A.A.
members were asked where they had gone for help (5). One-sixth
(17%) had been to clergy. So too had more than one-third (35%) of
our medical professionals—physicians, dentists, and nurses. Many
commented that they had found the clergyman no better informed
and no more helpful than medical people. Often plans were made
for less drinking, more church activity, perhaps some marital
counseling, but good intentions could not be kept and the project
was abandoned, usually with increased guilt and discouragement.
(We did not ask for this information from respondents in the
nonmedical professions.) When alcoholics told us that they sought
help from clergy, the presenting problem was often described in
terms of domestic or other conflicts with drinking mentioned, but
rarely seen as primary. In contrast, when one attends an A.A.
group, this signals that one either acknowledges being alcoholic
or is at least willing to consider the possibility.

MEDICAL TREATMENT

Many alcoholics believe initially that excessive drinking is symptomatic of an underlying emotional problem unique to the individual or that it is the result of some environmental stress.
Those who conceptualize the problem this way are likely to turn
to a mental health professional or to a trusted nonpsychiatric
physician able to identify the "real problem" and set it right—
perhaps through drug therapy, insight and understanding, a
change in geography, work habits, hobbies, or even marital arrangements.

Among the subjects of our study, contact with psychiatrists
was very common, and many remained in treatment for long
periods of time. More than two-fifths (43%) of them had seen one
or more psychiatrists before A.A. sobriety. In the New York City

study (5), 22 percent had sought help for their drinking problem from a psychiatrist before their A.A. contact. The data on outpatient treatment suggest that professional and better educated A.A. members are even more likely than others in A.A. to seek help from psychiatrists or the clergy for their drinking problems. Less than one-half of the New York City participants had attended college (49%) or had professional or managerial occupations (45%).

Other than clergy and physicians, relatively few professionals were consulted for help. Only 13 percent of our subjects went to psychologists or social workers, and many of these same subjects had sought physicians as well. There was widespread failure by both doctor and patient to recognize the signs of physical dependence on alcohol or the interrelationship among drinking, mood swings, and a variety of other complaints. Typically, physicians were approached with a host of different presenting problems—some physical, some emotional.

Just under one-quarter (23%) of the men, including 39 percent of the physicians, and one-tenth of the women reported that a treating person specifically denied that he or she was alcoholic. While listening to the physicians, it became clear that the usual pattern of interaction between treating person and patient had been that the patient would volunteer little or nothing about drinking and the treating person would not specifically ask about it. However, the physician-patient would sometimes minimize the problem or simply lie. We then devised a new set of questions for the other groups: "Did the treating person ever try to learn the truth about your drinking? Did you ever tell the whole truth about your drinking? When you told the whole truth, were you told you were *not* an alcoholic by the treating person?"

Since we did not ask all groups about this particular experience in the same way, we lost the opportunity to see if a psychiatrist was more likely to deny alcoholism in a fellow physician than in someone in another profession, as is suggested by the large number of physicians in our study who were told that they were *not* alcoholic. (In treating a peer, denial may be an attractive alternative to facing one's own vulnerability.) Perhaps the distancing effect of a difference in profession or sex makes it easier to suggest that a patient's problem is alcoholism, a diagnosis that is often accepted only intellectually and may feel at the time more like an accusation. Although the experiences of the physicians and the other groups cannot be compared, we do know that, when subjects claim to have told the whole truth about their drinking to a treating person, one-half (49%) of the men and one-fifth (19%) of the women said they still had their alcoholism specifically denied. As expected, many subjects reported that no treating person had sought the truth about their drinking. Predictably, a large number of these patients had also lied to at least one would-be helper.

Since the diagnosis of alcoholism was often made fairly late, made but not shared with the patient, or sometimes missed altogether, relatively few subjects reported being sent to A.A. or to a specialized alcoholism treatment facility. Instead, a great deal of time and effort was invested in trying to understand the reasons for drinking rather than in devising strategies for more direct intervention. This can be explained in part by the fact that the tremendous growth in clinics and residential facilities designed specifically for alcoholism and drug treatment is fairly recent. At the time that many of our subjects were undergoing treatment there were few such resources available, and those that existed were often not well known to either the patient or the therapist.

Systems for identifying the "impaired professional" were virtually nonexistent. There was little contact between those who understood alcoholics and those who needed treatment. There was not much room for optimism. This is not surprising considering that many of the treatment recommendations used then would now be regarded as actually destructive. Other addictive drugs were frequently and naively offered as substitutes for alcohol. Patients were urged to control rather than to stop drinking, and denial of alcoholism as the primary illness was commonplace. Sincere and sometimes desperate efforts to cooperate with inadequate or misdirected treatment were repeatedly described.

Hospital admissions often resulted from medical emergencies quite distinct from those planned for withdrawal from alcohol or other drugs, for other treatment of alcoholism itself, or for psychiatric investigation. Accidents were common. Seizures and gastrointestinal bleeding affected 18 percent and 15 percent of all subjects, respectively, and often led to, or complicated, hospitalization as did cirrhosis and other alcohol-related liver disease. These events contain the potential for diagnosis and referral for more definitive treatment of alcoholism, but this rarely follows for most such patients (6), and this was true for our subjects.

Plausible explanations were offered for the accidents that minimized the role of drinking and, even in retrospect, it would not always have been easy to suspect the truth. (One young psychiatrist described in some detail how he had swerved his car to avoid a doe and her fawn and had sustained his fracture while hitting a tree instead. His wife smiled in agreement as he embellished the story. Only the fact that this was his third hospital admission for trauma in three years could have raised suspicion.) Blood was rarely tested for alcohol concentration or for the presence of other drugs. Grand mal seizures were extensively evaluated by the most elaborate diagnostic techniques, but a thorough drinking and drug-use history was infrequently obtained. (In one author's personal experience as a clinician, the most common erroneous diagnoses previously assigned to middle- and upper-class alcoholic patients are idiopathic epilepsy, essential hypertension, and adult onset diabetes, most of which disappear or no longer require treatment when the drinking stops.)

When the presenting problem is pancreatitis, cirrhosis, or bleeding from the gastrointestinal tract, illnesses that every medical professional well knows are associated with heavy drinking, refusal to investigate further is harder to explain. Westermeyer et al. once investigated the prevalence of alcoholism in a population of private and semiprivate hospitalized patients, diagnosed them, and went on to offer help to their attending physicians at no additional cost and without any self-serving attempt to take over the case. The great majority of attending physicians, not patients, refused (7). The previously noted pattern of "Patient didn't volunteer, doctor didn't ask" appeared repeatedly. Even when family members, nurses who observed withdrawal symptoms in the professional patient, house staff, or other physicians were known to have tried to sound the alarm, they were often ignored.

One striking example involved an attorney admitted for open heart surgery to the hospital where his brother is a prominent member of the medical staff. He drank enormous quantities of vodka while entertaining family and friends, many of them also on the medical staff, in the days before surgery. Expressions of concern by a nurse and a resident were disregarded. After surgery, this man developed obvious delirium tremens and had an extremely complicated course. His physicians steadfastly refused even to consider that drinking was involved and, instead, talked at great length about sensory deprivation and the postcardiotomy syndrome.

Whether these avoidance behaviors are seen more frequently when the patient is a fellow professional than when he or she is not is still an open question. We did not distinguish different behaviors in different settings where a discussion of alcoholism or its denial might have come up. We do not know if physical evidence of drinking is ignored in the same way and for the same reasons as emotional or behavioral evidence, nor, if so, do we know if professionals are managed differently from other patients of similar socioeconomic class. The only certainty is that our subjects offered innumerable anecdotes of an almost global refusal on the part of all concerned to acknowledge and address their drinking.

As the toll of social and professional sanctions against our subjects increased, stays in institutions multiplied. Some went into hospitals repeatedly to "dry out" for short periods of time only to sign out again as early as possible, often against advice, and return to practice. Others agreed to long-term psychiatric hospitalization. (The inpatient experiences of the subjects are summarized in the previous chapter; see Table 4.2.)

One southern physician stayed nearly a year in a New England psychiatric hospital, during which time his alcoholism and drug use were barely mentioned while his "underlying problems" were addressed. No one suggested that he not drink after being discharged, and so on his way home he drank. The next day he consulted with a colleague "to see what I could take." He was reinstitutionalized within the week.

A married couple, a physician and nurse, who were both alcoholic and both physically dependent on alcohol, read of insulin shock as a possible cure for alcoholism. They drove to the treatment facility involved but decided the course of treatment would be too long. Accordingly they bought their own supply of insulin and intravenous glucose and spent a weekend in a motel drinking and giving each other insulin shock.

ALCOHOLICS ANONYMOUS

Expectations

A.A. is often perceived as essentially a religious organization and, indeed, its early history reveals its roots in both the Oxford Movement and the teachings of Carl Jung (8). Moreover, the press has reported the personal experiences of some of A.A.'s early members, several of whom describe undergoing profound religious conversion. Very few of our subjects had first heard of A.A. as part of their professional training (11 percent of the medical professionals, only one social worker, and no attorneys). Many of those who had heard of it were poorly informed or even misinformed. Some had been led to believe that it represents a somewhat suspect variety of folk medicine, while others gathered that it was a group of people who now substituted for the dependence on alcohol an equally unhealthy dependence on A.A. Some were wary of involvement with what they feared was a fanatic religious group or a group whose members were of a much lower social class than their own. Few had visited an A.A. meeting firsthand, even to explore it as a resource for others, and based their opinions entirely on hearsay or on popular media. Only a few were aware of knowing any A.A. members.

We asked specifically about their expectations, if any, concerning A.A.'s emphasis on religion before they approached the organization (see Table 5.1). Twelve percent said they had expected A.A.'s religious emphasis to "turn them off" and did find that this posed a problem. An almost equal number (10%) had similar expectations, but experienced no adverse effects. Forty-one percent did not expect this aspect to cause difficulty, and still another 37 percent reported not having any expectations about religion in A.A., one way or another. Thus, although just over one-fifth of the respondents had initially been reluctant to approach A.A. because of anticipated religious problems, half of that small group were pleasantly surprised. (This aspect did not appear to pose any greater problem for the Jewish respondents, although some of them reported that their belief that Jews are almost never alcoholic had delayed their acceptance of their alcoholism.) Still, it must be borne in mind that our respondents had chosen to become A.A. members. We know little of those who never approached A.A. or found it unacceptable and did not return.

Table 5.1 Expectation Regarding A.A. According to Sex

	All Subjects	Men	Women
$N =$	(362)[a]	(191)	(171)
A.A. emphasis on religion and adverse effects			
Expected it; had adverse effects	12%	11%	13%
Expected it; no adverse effects	10	11	9
Did not expect it	41	41	40
No expectations[b]	37	37	38
	100%	100%	100%
Socioeconomic level of A.A. members			
Higher than expected	41%	41%	40%
About what expected	3	2	3
Lower than expected	20	21	19
No expectations[b]	36	36	37
	100%	100%	100%

[a]Follow-up respondents only; items not asked to all professions in initial interview.
[b]Including 3 percent "don't know" or no answer.

Over one-third of the subjects said they had had no expectations concerning the socioeconomic status of A.A. members, while
two-fifths found people to be of higher status than anticipated
and one-fifth found them to be lower (Table 5.1). Only 3 percent
found about what they had expected to find. Men and women
reported having similar expectations regarding both the religious
emphasis in A.A. and the socioeconomic status of its members.

At first interview there was wide variation in the number of
A.A. meetings that individuals attended. This was influenced by
the size of the community, the availability of groups, whether a
spouse also belonged to A.A. or Alanon, and whether the respondent was involved in treating other alcoholics. Nonetheless,
97 percent of the 407 subjects said that they had attended A.A.
meetings one or more times in the previous year. (See Table 5.2.)
Three-fifths attended meetings at least once a week, and 5 percent
of these went to meetings daily.

Frequency of attendance was inversely related to the length of
abstinence. Those more newly sober tended to go to meetings
more frequently than those who had been abstinent for a longer
time (Table 5.2). Those who went to very few meetings were often

apologetic, saying they felt they probably should go more often and were anxious not to be seen as considering themselves good examples.

Its members do not refer to A.A. as "treatment," although outsiders often do. It is a fellowship in which there is little obvious power structure and in which members relate to one another as peers. One is not expected to complete a process, as one does with treatment; hence one is free to remain part of the group indefinitely without any need to finish a particular task or to advance in a hierarchy. No records are kept. There are no dues or fees. There are no patients and no therapists.

These various aspects of A.A. cannot be said either to have attracted or repelled our respondents, most of whom initially approached A.A. while knowing very little about it. Most knew only that it was supposed to help, but had only a vague idea of its methods. They were aware that its focus would be on drinking.

Outcome

All of our subjects eventually went to A.A. About one-half of them (men, 48%; women, 53%) reported at the intial interview that the first A.A. meeting and the last drink occurred at the same time. One-fifth reported no further drinking after their first year in A.A. (19% each for men and women). For the others

Table 5.2 Normal A.A. Attendance at Time of Initial Interview According to Length of Sobriety

		Length of Sobriety			
	All Subjects	1–2 Years	3–6 Years	7–12 Years	13 or more Years
A.A. Attendance $N =$	(407)	(122)	(150)	(79)	(56)
Daily	5%	5%	5%	4%	9%
2–6 times per week	37	52	36	29	21
Weekly	18	12	18	15	34
2–3 times per month	12	6	17	14	5
Monthly	21	22	19	27	16
11 times per year or less	4	—	3	9	11
Never	3	3	1	2	4
	100%	100%	100%	100%	100%

there were a series of exploratory visits and sometimes even
lengthy attendance punctuated with many relapses before a satisfactory alliance was made and the drinking ended.

Why did these professionals go to A.A. after what many described as a long period of resistance? These are some of the
reasons they gave:

"Left nursing. I loved it but I couldn't do it any more."
"My wife put Antabuse in my whiskey."
"I was sick as hell and didn't know what else to do."
"Lillian Roth's book."
"I just wanted to get sober for a while to protect my job."
"To keep the friendship of a patient who insisted I go."
"In jail."
"I hit a friend's little boy."
"They wouldn't let me adopt children."
"So tired of drinking, so many empty bottles in the office."
"Woke up and found I'd taken a Luger to bed with me."
"To preserve my marriage."
"Did surgery in a blackout."
"Drunk at my daughter's wedding."
"Husband unfaithful and I couldn't blame him."
"Afraid of losing custody of my child."
"Stranger in my bed in the morning."
"No place else to go."

Thus the decision usually came with a crisis, such as a threat
of job loss, the departure of an entire family, an episode of public
embarrassment, another drinking bout right after a hospitalization, the aftermath of a suicide attempt, or a feeling that there
really was no place else to go. Some went initially as a result of
pressure from others and planned only to go through the motions
until friends and family calmed down, but found something of
value and decided to remain.

Not all reported immediate cessation of drinking, and some
had a number of relapses, but 77 percent of the men and 74 percent
of the women indicated that there had been no relapse since the
end of the first year after joining A.A. (We defined "joining" as
having attended a total of 10 A.A. meetings, no matter how
distributed in time and regardless of the circumstances under
which they were attended.) Men were more likely than women to

cite family pressures as an event precipitating the A.A. contact (38% and 22%, respectively), but this doubtless reflects the difference in marital status and the men's greater likelihood of having an available spouse to exert pressure. Health problems were named by 28 percent of the women and 23 percent of the men. Economic pressures and professional difficulties were both mentioned about twice as often by men as women, and by the identical proportions of all subjects (17%, men; 9%, women).

Most subjects reported being comfortable around other drinkers; more than three-quarters (78%) of the men and two-thirds (68%) of the women serve alcoholic drinks in their homes (Table 5.3). Most socialize with other A.A. members, but 43 percent of the men and 26 percent of the women reported that other members of A.A. make up less than half of their friends.

Although we know that A.A. members tend to believe that a return to controlled or social drinking almost never works and should not be attempted, we wondered how much the ability to drink was missed. We asked the subjects if they thought that an alcoholic could ever return safely to social drinking. Almost all said no; a handful replied "very rarely" (Table 5.3). We then asked, if you *could* drink safely, would you? Only 26 percent said "yes," they would, while many volunteered that they felt relieved

Table 5.3 Serving and Drinking Alcoholic Beverages According to Sex

	All Subjects	Men	Women
$N =$	(407)	(207)	(193)
Serve alcoholic beverages at home	73%	78%	68%
Would, if could, drink safely	26%	18%	36%
Can alcoholic ever safely drink normally?			
No	88%	86%	91%
Yes or rarely	9	11	7
Undecided[a]	3	3	2
	100%	100%	100%

[a]Including 1 percent "don't know" or no answer.

rather than deprived by the absence of alcohol in their lives. Others made it very clear that "social drinking" did not appeal to them because they were interested only in drinking to feel the full effect. One attorney said that he would be no more interested in one or two drinks than in one or two salted peanuts. Fewer women than men thought it possible that an alcoholic could return safely to normal drinking, but twice as many women (36%) as men (18%) indicated that they would like to drink if it were safe.

Since ours is an A.A. sample, the respondents tended to give that organization the lion's share of credit for their recovery. However, they also pointed out that, although the medical care they received over the years did not necessarily address the alcohol problem, it did enable them to survive long enough to find a solution. The value of psychiatric care was heatedly debated. The consensus seems to be that treatment was of little use during active drinking because alcohol frequently causes an organic brain syndrome so severe that advice cannot be acted on or is sometimes completely forgotten. However, many felt that once drinking and drug effects were past and the habit of sobriety well established, psychiatric counseling in addition to, but not instead of, A.A. could work well. Twenty-eight percent of the medical professionals reported treatment after drinking had ceased and were still in treatment when first interviewed. (This information was not obtained from the other professionals.) A.A. and other help were seen as complementary by these subjects rather than as mutually exclusive, but timing, they agreed, was all important, with complete withdrawal from alcohol and other drugs to be addressed first.

Subjects frequently volunteered that there might actually be hazards involved in trusting a mental health professional who lacked specific expertise in treating alcoholics. The dangers most commonly mentioned were that the patient might be given another addictive drug, that there might be encouragement to attempt a return to controlled drinking, or that the therapist might elect to go into competition with A.A. and argue either that the A.A. group interfered with the treatment process or that it be regarded as an unhealthy substitute for the dependency on alcohol. If, on the other hand, the subject could decide to know better than the therapist specifically in those matters concerning A.A. and the use of alcohol and drugs, the therapist's advice could then be used quite constructively in dealing with all of the other human necessities that might need attention after the drinking had stopped. The subjects stressed repeatedly that most therapists were still far too ignorant about alcoholism and that even now the teaching, at least in medical schools, remains inadequate. Pokorny and Solomon's recent study would tend to confirm this impression (9).

REFERENCES

1. E. M. Smith et al., "Predictors of Mortality in Alcoholic Women: A Prospective Follow-Up Study," *Alcoholism: Clinical and Experimental Research 7*: 1983, pp. 237–43.

2. P. W. Haberman and M. M. Baden, *Alcohol, Other Drugs and Violent Death*, New York: Oxford University Press, 1978.

3. J. de Lint and I. Levinson, "Mortality among Patients Treated for Alcoholism: A Five-Year Follow-Up," *Canadian Medical Association Journal 113*: 1975, pp. 385–87.

4. B. B. Brenner, "Alcoholism and Fatal Accidents," *Quarterly Journal of Studies on Alcohol 28*: 1967, pp. 517–28.

5. M. B. Bailey et al., *Alcoholics Anonymous: Pathway to Recovery*, New York: National Council on Alcoholism, 1965.

6. S. E. Gitlow and H. Peyser, eds., *Alcoholism: A Practical Treatment Guide*, New York: Grune and Stratton, 1980.

7. J. Westermeyer et al., "An Assessment of Hospital Care of the Alcoholic Patient," *Alcoholism: Clinical and Experimental Research 2*: 1978, pp. 33–57.

8. E. Kurtz, *Not God: A History of Alcoholics Anonymous*, Minneapolis, Minn.: Hazelden, 1979.

9. A. D. Pokorny and J. Solomon, "Followup Survey of Drug Abuse and Alcoholism Teaching in Medical Schools," *Journal of Medical Education 58*: 1983, pp. 316–21.

6

Sobriety and Relapses

At the original interview we believed all of our subjects to be abstinent for at least a year and many for much longer. Accordingly, we expected that most would remain sober throughout the years between interviews but were curious to know if there would be changes in attitudes and behavior with more years of sobriety. We were also anxious to know which, if any, factors identified at the first interview might correlate with relapse.

There was little or no contact with any of the subjects between interviews other than for a single mailing to verify an address or an accidental encounter at a conference or convention. Nonetheless, people proved remarkably conscientious in telling us when they moved, and many kept track of each other and reported on moves and changes if they happened to know that a colleague was part of the study.

A few individuals initially interviewed were later dropped from the study and are not included in the results reported here. They illustrate the kind of problem encountered in work of this kind. Of the physician sample, one subject was not abstinent long enough at the time of the first interview to qualify and acknowledged this only at his follow-up interview. A second man was not a physician at all and proved instead to be a podiatrist who enjoyed the company of physicians and reportedly never had trouble passing himself off as one of them. A third was Australian and unlikely after his decision to return home to be available for a second interview. In all groups, whenever there was any doubt of the subject's eligibility, the person was dropped. Several interviews had to be discarded altogether when an interviewer was suspected of fabricating results. Our original plan to have tidy numbers of exactly 100 or 50 in each group was altered as this attrition took place, and hence we decided to enlarge all subsequent groups to include "extras." Thus we report on 97 physicians, 49 dentists, but have samples of 55 attorneys and 56 college women.

We permitted ourselves to be persuaded that having women physicians and male nurses would be "averaging apples and oranges" and that they should be excluded. Wrong! We should have gotten the information and handled statistics in a different way as needed. Since the handful of other investigators who have studied these professions have done the same thing, we all remain almost totally ignorant of the alcoholic woman physician or the male nurse and cannot even pool information about the ones who could have been studied. They were there but we were not receptive.

It has been the common wisdom that alcoholics are hard to locate for follow-up studies—an assumption that provides yet another convenient excuse for the paucity of good studies on treatment outcome (1,2). When subjects are located, the veracity of their self-reports has been questioned and confirmation sought from presumably more reliable family members (3). Interestingly enough, Kammeier found little difference in reports of drinking whether offered by the alcoholic or the spouse, but noted that an A.A. sponsor was less likely to report that his "pigeon" was drinking than was the alcoholic to tell on his or her own self (4).

There has also been a tacit assumption that an alcoholic refusing follow-up, one who has died, or one who cannot be located must have been drinking, an automatic "no news is bad news" posture that reflects and tends to reinforce the pessimism about treatment that has plagued this field. If these assumptions are true and if every possible effort is made to locate all subjects, then those who prove hardest to find or to have died should be much more likely to have relapsed than those who are readily

available. In addition, those with the longest time periods between interviews would have additional time in which to get into
trouble.

We were able to locate for in-person reinterview nearly nine-
tenths of the original sample. We considered as successfully followed up all those whom we interviewed a second time in person
or for whom we had a full face-to-face or telephone interview
with a very close relative. We regarded as only partially followed
up those who did not have such family members, even though
close friends often gave excellent information and were probably
at times even more reliable than relatives. Blood relatives and
legal next of kin often knew little about the subjects, frequently
were unaware that alcoholism, much less a research project, had
ever existed, and were anxious to protect the family reputation
and to get rid of inquisitive strangers. When the original decision
to accept telephone contact with relatives but not with alcoholics
was taken, it was in order to observe firsthand any signs of alcohol
or other drug use by the subjects. Presumably spouses and other
relatives were not alcoholic and these considerations were not
necessary. Wrong again. Alcoholics do marry other alcoholics,
and both partners in a marriage do not always recover together.

While obtaining the original interviews was fairly easy since
many could be done in a short period of time at conferences
and conventions, follow-ups were much more difficult. People
retired, moved, married, or just stayed home more and stopped
going to so many meetings. They enlarged their practices, got
busy, went on with their lives. They remained cooperative but
unlikely to travel very far in order to accommodate interviewers
who wanted face-to-face contact. We had to go to them or lose
the face-to-face format. We went to them. At least two interviews classified as "refusals" might have been obtained, but
geography, expenses, and scheduling difficulties forced us to
abandon the attempt. Whenever repeated efforts to arrange an
interview failed and the subject's behavior made subsequent approaches seem equally unlikely to succeed, these have also been
called "refusals," behavioral or indirect rather than verbal or
direct.

We were finally able to obtain at least some information on all
but 7 of our original 407. While, of course, these 7 may all have
returned to drinking, for all the others we have at least partial

information. The hard-to-locate proved no more likely to have relapsed than the others, and those who had died had for the most part remained sober as well. (See Table 6.1.)

Refusal to grant the second interview also did not seem to indicate a relapse into drinking. We have information on 9 of the 15 refusals; 8 of these were probably sober after the initial interview (Table 6.1). It may be worth noting that, while less than a dozen of the original sample reported ever having taken lithium, 3 of those who refused were taking it at the original interview. Others who refused or had others refuse for them included 2 who were in the terminal stage of chronic illness, an elderly physician now residing in a nursing home and rather unlikely to be drinking, though he did not wish to be bothered with us, and a male social worker who was angry at one of the investigators who had refused to hire him during the follow-up period. This man saw a chance to get even by denying the interview and said as much. A nurse held us somehow responsible for her being on a mailing list that she found annoying and she wanted no more to do with us. Another nurse had joined a fundamentalist church where all of her fellow church members were also abstainers. She stated that she had "found God," no longer attended A.A., and wanted no reminder of it or of her previous problems.

Of the 7 that could not be found at all, 5 were women, 4 of them nurses. At least 2 were rumored to have married and moved away, and had probably changed their names. State licensing agencies had no records. With the wisdom of hindsight, we realized that we should have discussed with these nurses the best people through whom to locate them if they were to move and then prove hard to trace. We did not do this with the health-care professionals; instead, we asked for next of kin, people who might predecease or even move together with the subject, and so we lost touch. An additional problem was failure to obtain permission to use other contacts, such as alumni offices of professional schools, an excellent source from which to learn a graduate's whereabouts, but where a show of interest from people known to work in the alcoholism field might cast suspicion on the subject. (One man while agreeing to be interviewed insisted on meeting in a delicatessen remote from home and hospital because to be seen with the investigator was "like having two scarlet letters around my neck!")

Table 6.1 Probable Drinking Status after Initial Interview of Subjects Not Reinterviewed

Probable Drinking Status after Initial Interview	Total Not Reinterviewed $N = 50$	Reason for No Reinterview[a]		
			Deceased	
		Refused	Significant Person Reinterviewed	Partial or No Information
Drinking	14%	1	4	2
Sober	60%	8	9[b]	13
No information	26%	6	—	7
	100%	15	13	22

[a]Excluding seven subjects who could not be located
[b]Including one case with partial information (data missing).

100

DEATHS

As shown in Table 6.2, a total of 35 subjects died before they were due for a second interview, 2 so soon and unexpectedly after the first contact that insisting on a follow-up interview with the surviving spouse seemed pointless. For 13 of these, interviews were obtained with a significant person fully conversant with the subject's history since first contact, usually the spouse. For 22 others, no appropriate person could be identified or the interview was refused.

Distant relatives were, as previously stated, often more protective than the deceased had been about himself or herself in the sharing of information. Still we learned quite a bit as we tried to find relatives; for those who seemed to disappear, it was tempting to accept as valid rumors about what may have happened. For example, one dentist was said by colleagues to have been "drinking and drugging" and to have gone off to a Sunbelt state with someone else's wife. He died violently soon afterwards. Two women were known to be in treatment for cancers that carried a poor prognosis when first interviewed. Since certainty about these deaths is impossible, we have simply grouped them as "probably drinking," "probably not drinking," or "information too limited" even to guess. In this study as well as in the recent study by Smith et al. (5) on causes of death in women alcoholics, death was more closely correlated with advanced age at first contact than with any other single factor, an observation so obvious that it may escape mention.

PREVIOUS STUDIES

Most of the relatively few published reports on treatment outcome for alcoholic professionals are limited to those concerned with male physicians, with now and then a few dentists (6,7) or nurses (8) included. Studies often report only whether or not the former patient is still alive, still licensed, or in practice (9,10,11).

If treatment "success" is regarded as synonymous with continued ability to work rather than defined in terms of abstinence, little information may be obtained about drinking per se. More sought after may be evidence of freedom from additional arrests, suicide attempts, hospitalizations, and inappropriate drug use.

Table 6.2 Follow-Up Rate According to Profession and Sex

	All Subjects	Profession						Sex	
		Physicians	Dentists	Nurses	Attorneys	Social Workers	College Women	Men	Women
Initial interview	407	97	49	100	55	50	56	214	193
Deceased	35	12	9	6	4	1	3	25	10
Significant person reinterviewed	13[a]	8	1	1	1	1[a]	1	10	3[a]
Partial or no information	22	4	8	5	3	—	2	15	7
Follow-up sample $N =$	372	85	40	94	51	49	53	189	183
Reinterviewed[b]	94%	98%	100%	92%	92%	86%	98%	96%	92%
Refused	4%	2%	—	4%	6%	10%	2%	3%	5%
Not located	2%	—	—	4%	2%	4%	—	1%	3%
	100%	100%	100%	100%	100%	100%	100%	100%	100%

[a]Including one case with partial information (data missing).
[b]Including both direct and indirect (inferred) refusals.

Stability of residence, job, and marriage, as well as successful integration into a mutual help group, have also been considered, but we know little of any of these outcomes among professional groups. Controls or even simple comparisons with other patient groups undergoing similar treatment in the same facility are also rare (12). Furthermore, when there is no clear indication of what goal was attempted, it is hard to judge the result.

More serious problems stem from what is often a much too brief follow-up period. The longer the time since treatment, the more time there is in which to relapse. Even without treatment, many alcoholics can abstain for weeks or months while still others are able to drink for prolonged periods without major difficulty before control is lost again and trouble follows.

Small et al. report an Indiana University Medical Center study of 40 mentally ill physicians who were matched with other hospitalized professionals as controls (13). While physicians claimed to have maintained their occupational responsibilities quite well prior to admission, they did poorly in terms of family adjustment. Other professionals manifested the reverse findings in these "social adjustment" ratings.

Recently, there have been studies in which goals of treatment as well as results have been more explicitly stated. They come as something of a relief after the rather frightening treatment outcome ("success" in only 17 of 41 physicians who were chemical abusers) reported by Murray for physicians treated for alcoholism at a London psychiatric hospital where it is unclear whether abstinence was urged or exactly what staff had set for themselves to accomplish as goals (14). It is tempting to believe that the marked contrast in success in treating physicians, reported now as compared to the past, derives from certain changes in how patients are motivated for treatment and in the messages given them during treatment itself. More and more, colleagues are making it clear to the alcoholic that drunken behavior is no longer to be tolerated, that the problem is seen as an illness rather than a personal weakness or failure, and that, with recovery, full rehabilitation is not only possible but expected. During treatment it is emphasized that the patient's drinking is to stop altogether— not merely be explained and understood. Other drugs of addiction are to be avoided. There is more willingness to work with and complement A.A. rather than to compete with it or to "cop out" to it. It may well be that, for professionals as well as other alcoholics, the days are numbered when we can "blame the victim" for the many inadequacies of treatment. Alcoholics have long been considered hard to treat because they were thought to be unmotivated. Presumably no one could help until the alcoholic was "ready" or had "hit bottom." Now it is known that creating motivation is part of the intervention-treatment process. Perhaps we will discover that, just as alcoholic women can respond well when appropriate treatment is used, as can men, professionals may also be shown to be fully able to recover when sensible treatment is offered.

In 1979, Goby et al. conducted telephone follow-up interviews with 43 of the 51 physician patients treated over a 10-year period (mean of 42 months since release) at Lutheran General Hospital (LGH) in Illinois (15). Of the original group, 1 was incarcerated and 7 had died. (One of the deceased committed suicide, 1 died abstinent of lung cancer, 3 died drinking excessively, and the cause of death for 2 could not be ascertained.) Nineteen (44%) were abstinent since discharge; 9 more had done some drinking but were abstinent for a full year or more at follow-up. Only 8 failed to show a marked decrease in their drinking pattern. Since 4 died while still drinking, presumably heavily, 12 (24%) were not improved. Most reported good physical and emotional health and were working. Physicians represented 0.5 percent of the 10,000 patients treated in this period and did not differ significantly from other LGH alcoholism patients.

In 1980, Morse (16) reported on 53 surviving patients who had been treated for at least two weeks at the Mayo Clinic and who could be reached for follow-up. One to five years after discharge, 83 percent of the physicians compared to 62 percent of a non-physician "general group" had a favorable outcome (defined as abstinent altogether or having been in relapse for no more than one week as well as abstinent when contacted).

Also in 1980, Kliner et al. (17) did a questionnaire study by mail of 67 physicians treated at Hazelden one year after discharge. (The spouse or significant other was also asked to respond.) Of the 57 who replied, 51 reported abstinence since discharge, 5 had experienced serious difficulty with continued drinking, and 1 other reported continued drinking but no related problems. This group also reported improvements in self-image, health, professional performance, and personal adjustment. Patients in both the Morse (16) and Kliner studies also reported a high rate of affiliation with A.A., Narcotics Anonymous (NA), or both.

In 1981, Johnson and Connelly (6) followed 43 physicians and 7 dentists addicted to alcohol and/or other drugs treated at the Menninger Clinic for 9 to 54 months and reported 64 percent improvement. In 1982, Herrington et al. (7) reported on 40 doctors treated in Wisconsin. Seven dropped out of treatment early, but of the 30 physicians and 3 dentists who remained, 22 were abstinent since discharge and 6 more had had only a single relapse. About 94 percent were in practice. Also in 1982, Shore (12) reported that 22 out of 27 alcoholic or drug-addicted physicians in monitored treatment in Oregon under state board supervision were improved, with 14 reporting no relapse. Probation had lasted from 1 to 120 months (mean 3.6 years).

Both Herrington and Shore pointed out that those addicted to narcotics did no worse than those addicted to alcohol alone (7,12). Smith (18) has pointed out that narcotic addiction in professionals has been quite different from that of the street addict. Use starts later, and the drugs are obtained through different channels, are pure, strong, and predictable. Use is in isolation. There is no physician drug culture. As he puts it, "You don't see several addicted doctors shooting up together in the back room of a hospital as you might see young people do in a flat in the Haight Ashbury." Thus, the addicted physician can give up narcotics without also having to give up a whole life-style and social group. For the professional, it is the giving up of alcohol that requires the alteration of social patterns. There is no rejection for stopping other drug use, but when a former drinking companion becomes an abstainer, many changes occur.

DRINKING DURING THE FOLLOW-UP PERIOD

In its 1980 membership survey, A.A. predicted that a randomly selected member with one to five years' sobriety has an 86 percent chance of completing the next year without drinking and a 92 percent chance if already sober over five years. Only 41 percent of those sober less than a year are predicted to get through the subsequent year without drinking and, of the "newcomers," only half, sober or not, remain in A.A. more than three months (19).

If the above is true, then our subjects with a median sobriety of six years when first interviewed might be expected to show a rate of attrition of about 8 percent per year. Of our own subjects, four-fifths of those for whom follow-up interviews were obtained reported complete abstinence from alcohol during the entire period. There was no particular difference in drinking between the men and women.

We had expected that almost all who returned to any drinking would continue to drink until back in serious trouble again. Instead, we heard people describe what seemed to be two quite different experiences. Table 6.3 shows drinking during follow-up, with those who relapsed divided into those who drank on a total of four days or less and those who drank on five or more occasions. Obviously, any drinking at all is not the ideal for a group endorsing total abstinence as their goal, but those who on average drank on less than one day per year may well be regarded as quite different from those who drank frequently. Those currently drinking or admitting to drinking in the 60 days preceding the interview we regarded as still drinking.

Among those who relapsed were 27 (7%) who drank on only four or even fewer occasions, no more on average than once a year, and in some cases only once or twice altogether—a small but interesting group. They frequently described the drinking experience as an impulsive one, perhaps occurring at a wedding or when sharing in a toast seemed somehow unavoidable. These were not planned drinking episodes, were sometimes experienced as quite dysphoric, often did not involve enough intake for any perceptible mood change, and were not followed by any particular desire to go on drinking. These individuals seemed quite different from many of the others who returned to more extensive and frequently disastrous drinking. However, not all of those who drank only on rare occasions escaped trouble. The only man, an attorney, who attempted suicide during the follow-up period did so on the single occasion when he drank, while one nurse who had been experimenting with tranquilizers accidentally overdosed when she added alcohol as well.

The 46 (13%) who drank on five or more occasions were more likely to describe toying with the idea of drinking, experimenting rather cautiously, then finding that there no longer seemed to be a problem with control (Table 6.3). Pleased and relieved to discover

Table 6.3 Drinking and Drug Use between Interviews According to Profession and Sex

	All Subjects N = (362)	Profession						Sex	
		Physicians (91)	Dentists (41)	Nurses (87)	Attorneys (48)	Social Workers (42)	College Women (53)	Men (191)	Women (171)
Drinking between interviews									
Five or more days	13%	19%	5%	13%	8%	14%	11%	12%	14%
One to four days	7	9	10	8	2	5	10	7	8
Abstinent	80	72	85	79	90	81	79	81	78
	100%	100%	100%	100%	100%	100%	100%	100%	100%
Drinking at follow-up	3%	7%	—	1%	2%	5%	2%	3%	3%
Drug trouble between interviews[a]	12%	21%	12%	10%	13%	7%	4%	15%	9%
Drug trouble at follow-up	2%	4%	—	3%	2%	—	2%	2%	3%

[a]Excluding 2 of 46: 1 physician and 1 female social worker without reinterviews.

themselves again able to drink socially, they attempted to do just that until they were back in trouble. Some did this several times, but all but 3 percent of the total surviving subjects had been abstinent for at least two months prior to the second interview.

One physician whose long-standing drinking history would satisfy the criteria for alcoholism of even the most exacting investigator and who had remained abstinent in A.A. for six years before his original interview stated at second interview that he had returned to social drinking about a year after that first contact, no longer attended A.A., and had experienced no difficulty related to his resumed drinking over at least a four-year period. He had married, now drank only with his wife as opposed to his original "bar with the boys" pattern, had exchanged a demanding private practice for a fixed-income situation, and had made other alterations in his life-style. When asked if he still considered himself "alcoholic," he said, "I don't know. I must have been." Of the very few who reported current drinking at the time of the second interview, he was the only one apparently not in trouble. After very careful investigation we have found no reason to doubt the honesty of his report, even though such successful returns to "social drinking" are rare.

OTHER DRUGS

At first interview, more than three-fifths of the men (63%) and women (65%) gave a history of addiction to alcohol alone, the others having been addicted to one or more additional drugs. (See Chapter 2.) At follow-up, 48 percent of the men and 56 percent of the women acknowledged some drug use during the interval, with 22 percent of each sex still reporting some current use. "Use" as reported here does not mean that these drugs have caused problems. It does mean that potentially dangerous drugs were used, whether or not they were used rarely or legally obtained. Most common was the use of minor tranquilizers, allegedly without difficulty.

DRUG USE BETWEEN INTERVIEWS

At the initial interview, 21 percent of the physicians, nurses, and dentists said they were currently using one or more mood-changing drugs. (The nonmedical groups were not asked this question.) None felt themselves to be addicted to any drug being used at that time. Most drugs were described as used infrequently, were in small doses, or were being taken under a physician's supervision. We hypothesized that anyone continuing to use drugs, no matter how innocently, would be more prone to a relapse into drinking and would also be more likely to have problems with the drugs themselves. Not only had this been our clinical experience but, particularly in the case of sedative use, it seemed unlikely that recovery from the addiction to alcohol would be long sustained by substituting another similar addictive drug. Quite aside from pursuing a misdirected search for solutions to human problems solely through chemical answers, the subject would be experiencing sedation followed by increased agitation and would therefore ultimately face increased discomfort. Relief would be temporary at best.

The relationship of other drug use and subsequent drinking has been discussed above. The question of drug use and its relationship to more trouble with drugs per se is less clear. Those who were using drugs at first interview had not initially made a commitment to stop usage. They were not going to solve what they did not see as a problem, and the interviewers attempted not to show any approval or disapproval. We could then be certain that many would report at least some continued use, whether or not it was followed by difficulties. A total of 77 (26 women and 51 men) did use potentially addicting drugs outside of hospitals during the follow-up period. Of this group, 60 percent (16 women and 30 men) went on to experience serious difficulties (Table 6.3). The rest claimed to have stopped before there were problems or continued to use and denied any problems.

Of the 46 having or reporting drug trouble between interviews, 18 (39%) had also relapsed into drinking—many then using both other drugs and alcohol at the same time. We asked about hospitalizations for alcohol or drug problems and exactly half (23) had been hospitalized. Together they had 29 hospitalizations that are clearly enumerated. One physician who continued drugging himself and drinking until his death at age 64 was said by his son also to have been hospitalized "many times," and another physician spent 3 months in a halfway house.

A long history of addiction to drugs other than alcohol was not uncommon in the 46 who had trouble. Twenty had initially reported addiction to alcohol only, but 10 had histories of addiction to "hard" narcotics as well as to nonnarcotics (6 physicians, 3 nurses, and 1 female social worker—nearly one-third of all of those reporting "hard" narcotics addiction at first interview), while 16 had been addicted to nonnarcotic prescription drugs. Eighteen (10 women and 8 men) were subjects who had also reported suicide attempts prior to the first interview. There were no additional attempts reported. Three died before the second interview: the physician mentioned above; a dentist whose Valium use was followed by drinking, the loss of his license, and death, officially by myocardial infarction; and a social worker, said by her husband to have been entirely free of drugs and alcohol for two years before her death.

Almost all of the people who had trouble with one drug during the follow-up period had trouble with other drugs as well. This was true of three who developed or redeveloped addiction to Demerol and also of an additional three addicted to Talwin. All six of these (4 physicians and 2 nurses) had reported narcotic addiction prior to the first interview as well, though all were evidently not using drugs when initially interviewed.

Another nurse, also a previous narcotic addict, was hospitalized on three separate occasions for treatment of an orthopedic problem. Each time she was treated with Darvon and Valium for pain and muscle spasm. Each time she lost control of her drug intake, used ever-increasing amounts of both drugs, and each time had to be admitted elsewhere for detoxification. She was again drug free at second interview and determined to accept even extreme physical discomfort, if need be, rather than risk reactivating her addiction. A dentist with no previous history of drug use was self-prescribing large amounts of codeine at follow-up, and one of the educated women who had acknowledged frequent use of Valium or Dalmane at first interview was found to be taking generous amounts of Darvon, Vistaril, Donnatal, meprobamate, codeine, and amphetamine.

The last two subjects mentioned above are among those whom we have included as having trouble with drugs. This can of course be challenged. For the purposes of this study, we are defining "trouble" as having experienced clearly adverse consequences associated with the drugs, being obviously intoxicated or bizarre at the interview, or otherwise appearing to a skilled interviewer as being on the verge of serious trouble. There are obvious dilemmas here that have regularly plagued those who read about addiction. Terms like "addiction" itself, "use," "abuse," and "misuse" are often so poorly defined as to render many studies impossible to interpret.

One of our physicians at follow-up was using Librium, Quaalude, LSD, hashish, marijuana, and cocaine. He did not feel he had a drug problem. His interviewer thought he did. She based her assessment on the quantities used, his attitude, and the marked change in his demeanor since she previously interviewed him, but not necessarily on his choice of drugs alone or on the fact that some of them are illegal. If *all* use of illegal drugs is by definition "abuse" or "misuse" and these terms are taken to mean the person is "in trouble" as well, then more than 46 of our subjects got into "trouble." If any self-prescribing of psychotropics or using them in excess of recommended dosage is "misuse," then we would have to include still more subjects. If a drug is legal but thought to be more addictive than others that might serve the same function—that is, Doriden or Quaalude rather than perhaps a benzodiazepine—users of these too may be regarded with suspicion.

Subjects were quite open with our interviewers, or at least we believed them to be. Inevitably some users were back in the denial phase, and we have included several who could not or did not see themselves at risk. Some of these included a physician regularly using Demerol, codeine, hashish, and barbiturates; two college women using large quantities of amphetamine plus an assortment of other drugs; a social worker who had been using Fiorinal occasionally for sleep when first interviewed, went on to add meprobamate, next returned to drinking, and then was hospitalized. She is now drinking heavily again and has a physician prescribing large amounts of Librium for her. She does not exceed the amount he prescribes. Two attorneys at first interview said they had previously been addicted—one to Serax, one to Valium. Both admitted to continued, occasional use at that time. Both are now regular heavy users, but deny any problem.

Obtaining prescription drugs has evidently not been difficult, whether or not one works in the health-care field. The typical drug experience as described by our professionals might go as follows: The subject accepts that drinking must stop altogether, but is not told or is not convinced that there is any danger in taking an occasional minor tranquilizer for sleep or a particularly stressful event. More or less innocently, the drug is used and it works. This is not seen as a major event and it is not immediately followed by any adverse consequences. Repeated but infrequent use demonstrates that there is nothing to fear. Experience shows the drug to be safe, so regular use becomes acceptable so long as the medication is taken in moderation. Still no problem. Gradually tolerance builds, so that when the drug is discontinued or not available a rebound increase in anxiety occurs. (Significant physical dependency has been reported even at recommended doses of benzodiazepines.) Withdrawal of the drug now provokes enough agitation that its presence seems to establish that the drug is indeed needed and justifies its continued use (20). Sleep disturbance becomes the norm but is not consciously related to the drug.

Alcohol, an excellent tranquilizer, remains omnipresent and may begin to seem more attractive as A.A. becomes less so. A.A. members are seen as too bigoted and intolerant about pills. They urge members not to take them. They are not skilled pharmacologists and need to appreciate that treatment should be individualized and that a professional, after all, knows quite a lot about drugs and has sense enough to get them from a physician (even if the physician is oneself!). Rather than hear them scold, people at A.A. are no longer told about the drugs. That information now remains secret. No longer places in which to share freely, the A.A. meetings become less rewarding, frequency of attendance drops, and there is now more time available to spend with others, usually people who drink and who certainly do not need to be alienated by being told about alcoholism or shocked by stories of a best-forgotten past.

At this stage the story varies but usually goes in one of three directions. Sooner or later, many reach for the seemingly harmless drink and the romance with alcohol begins again, the previous struggle and separation almost forgotten. The other drug may then be dropped altogether in favor of the first love, alcohol. Or there may be a slow but steady increase in the use of the drug itself with no concomitant drinking, but with the new drug becoming a major problem in its own right. (Three of our subjects who did not return to drinking required hospitalization for dependency on Valium.) Even more common is that alcohol is simply added and now both it and the other drug or drugs are used simultaneously. Often pills are used during the day when the odor of alcohol might be detected and the drinking is done at night.

The effect of alcohol and tranquilizers in combination can be tricky to regulate, and the combination of alcohol and a benzodiazepine tranquilizer is the most common form of drug overdose requiring emergency room treatment in the United States today (21). The social worker mentioned above was also hospitalized for a serious overdose when she became impatient with the slowness with which her Valium was taking effect and gulped some vodka to hasten the process. (Her physician then stopped her Valium and began giving her Librium instead!)

The experience of our subjects confirms that the use of other mood-changing drugs by alcoholic people carries with it significant danger. If an antipsychotic drug such as phenothiazine or lithium is required for a major emotional illness, it both could and should be given. The drugs that are the least necessary are the ones that appear to be most likely to cause trouble: the soporifics, minor tranquilizers, stimulants, and certain of the slow-acting mood elevators that have a significant tranquilizing action as a side effect. Obviously narcotics may have to be used for severe pain and given in adequate amounts, but they should be discontinued as rapidly as possible.

SUICIDE

Thirty percent of the women and 17 percent of the men had made overt suicide attempts prior to the initial interview. (See Chapter 4.) In the ensuing five to seven years, only three women and one man, an attorney, did so. The attorney had made an attempt prior to first interview. He drank impulsively on a single occasion and then deliberately overdosed with sedatives. A social worker, not a previous attempter, did not drink or use drugs but had experienced a reactive depression. The other two were college women, both of whom had also made previous attempts. These two had used alcohol or other drugs, or both, during the followup period, and both were drinking when the actual attempts were made—one using a gun, the other using sedatives. One reported five previous attempts—three overdoses, an episode of wrist slashing, and an attempt at suffocating herself in a plastic bag.

An additional subject, a nurse, while remaining abstinent from alcohol, did resume the use of sedatives and died of an intentional overdose. She was said to have been involved in a turbulent romantic entanglement at the time. About three years after the second round of interviews, we were told by a reliable woman of the probable suicide of a recently retired physician. The informant wanted us to know that he had not resumed drinking and had taken pains to learn about that aspect of the case, but no other details were offered.

ARRESTS

While, as previously noted, one-fifth (19 percent) of the women and half (49 percent) of the men reported arrests prior to the initial interview, only three women and six men had been arrested during the period between interviews. Two of these women were nurses and both of them had been drinking. One was charged with reckless driving, the other with driving while intoxicated (DWI). The men included five physicians and one dentist. Again, alcohol was very much involved with three separate arrests for DWI, two for speeding, one for possession of a gun (which was waved during a drinking bout), and one for assault ("I spanked someone else's child!"). The only other arrest involved a social worker carried off to jail during a peace demonstration. She had been sober at the time, described the episode with satisfaction, and was firm in her intention of being arrested again if need be in what she saw as a good cause.

HOSPITALIZATION

At first interview all subjects were asked if they had ever been institutionalized for alcoholism or an alcohol-related illness, regardless of what it was called at the time (Chapter 4). (This was essentially a lifetime experience, not limited to a discrete period before either a decrease or cessation of drinking.) We also asked about any alcohol- or drug-related admissions, as well as admissions that were not alcohol- or drug-related between the two interviews. Prior to the first interview, the 407 subjects combined had accounted for 3.8 alcohol-related admissions per subject—a total of over 1,500 admissions!

During the follow-up period, only 1.1 admissions per subject for all reasons were reported. Only 16 percent of these hospitalizations were for alcoholism or other drug-related problems, and some admissions did not even indicate ill health. One nurse listed three admissions for normal childbirth, and several men and women had cosmetic surgery for revision of scars earned during their drinking years. Others were admitted for procedures previously recommended but long postponed, such as hernia operations and removal of impacted teeth.

DISCUSSION

It is not surprising that, when abstinence was maintained, arrests, suicide attempts, and hospitalizations (even though the subjects were now older) were markedly decreased. We had hoped to identify those factors found at initial interview that might indicate the likelihood of relapse. Since only 13 percent of the total group *did* drink five or more days between interviews, we have only 46 to study and conclusions must be cautious.

The factors observed in the initial interview that were associated with a poor prognosis are indicated in Table 6.4. By profession, physicians were most likely to relapse. Unexpectedly, relapses occurred most often among those subjects whose parents were *not* reported to be alcoholics, and least often among those whose fathers were alcoholics. A history of addiction to other drugs, nonnarcotics in particular, was positively correlated with drinking between interviews.

Those respondents who had said that they would drink if they could do so "safely" were more likely than the others to relapse. Similarly, those who believed or were undecided about whether an alcoholic can ever return safely to normal drinking relapsed more frequently than those who did not believe this. Those subjects who believed that alcoholism is primarily mental, emotional, or psychological relapsed more often than those who favored physical or biochemical theories of alcoholism.

As anticipated, those subjects who in the initial interview reported having had one or more slips since their first year in A.A. were most likely to slip again between interviews, whereas those who had never had a slip since they became A.A. members most often remained completely abstinent. Sobriety between interviews was also directly related to years of sobriety and to chronological age at the time of the first interview.

We have described those subjects who on average drank less than once a year during a five-year period between interviews as being quite different from the ones who drank more frequently.

Table 6.4 Selected Factors Associated with Drinking between Interviews

Associated Factors from Initial Interview $N =$	Reported Drinking between Interviews		
	None (289)	One to Four Days (27)	Five or More Days (46)
Profession as a physician	23%	30%	37%
Parental alcoholism			
Father	24%	33%	13%
Mother	6	4	4
Both parents	6	7	7
Neither parent	64	56	76
	100%	100%	100%
History of addiction to mood-altering drugs other than "hard" narcotics	27%	33%	39%
Attitudes toward drinking and alcoholism			
Would, if could drink "safely"	24%	33%	43%
Responded "yes," "rarely," or "undecided" that alcoholic can ever return safely to normal drinking	9%	19%	22%
Alcoholism is primarily mental, emotional, or psychological[a]	24%	22%	37%
Slips since A.A.			
None at all	60%	44%	41%
None since first year	19	19	22
One or more since first year	21	37	37
	100%	100%	100%
Years of sobriety			
One to two	25%	41%	50%
Three to six	37	37	41
Seven or more	38	22	9
	100%	100%	100%
Age			
25–39	16%	22%	39%
40–54	54	52	33
55 and over	30	26	28
	100%	100%	100%

[a]Follow-up interview; item not asked in initial interview.

However, on most of the factors discussed here, the percents for those who drank fewer than five days between interviews were in the middle range of the percents for those who reported no drinking at all or drinking on five or more occasions at follow-up. Two other items in the initial interview that we had expected might be related to subsequent drinking by respondents were infrequent attendance at A.A. and failure to seek treatment outside of A.A. However, drinking between interviews did not vary appreciably according to A.A. attendance or whether there had also been professional treatment.

REFERENCES

1. C. D. Emrick, "A Review of Psychologically Oriented Treatment of Alcoholism: I. The Use and Interrelationships of Outcome Criteria and Drinking Behavior Following Treatment," *Quarterly Journal of Studies on Alcohol 35*: 1974, pp. 523–49.

2. ———, "A Review of Psychologically Oriented Treatment of Alcoholism: II. The Relative Effectiveness of Different Treatment Approaches and the Effectiveness of Treatment versus No Treatment," *Journal of Studies on Alcohol 36*: 1975, pp. 88–109.

3. N. G. Hoffman et al., "Alcoholics Anonymous after Treatment: Attendance and Abstinence," *International Journal of the Addictions 18*: 1983, pp. 311–18.

4. Sr. M. L. Kammeier, Personal Communication, 1977.

5. E. M. Smith et al., "Predictors of Mortality in Alcoholic Women: A Prospective Follow-Up Study," *Alcoholism: Clinical and Experimental Research 7*: 1983, pp. 237–43.

6. R. P. Johnson and J. C. Connelly, "Addicted Physicians, A Closer Look," *Journal of the American Medical Association 245*: January 16, 1981, pp. 253–57.

7. R. E. Herrington et al., "Treating Substance-Use Disorders among Physicians," *Journal of the American Medical Association 247:* April 23–30, 1982, pp. 2253–58.

8. M. M. Glatt, "Alcoholism and Drug Dependence in Doctors and Nurses," *British Medical Journal*, February 10, 1968, pp. 380–81.

9. M. P. Brook et al., "Psychiatric Illness in the Medical Profession," *British Journal of Psychiatry 113*: April 23–30, 1967, pp. 1013–23.

10. R. A. Franklin, "One Hundred Doctors at the Retreat," *British Journal of Psychiatry 131*: 1977, pp. 11–14.

11. G. D. Talbott et al., "The Medical Association of Georgia's Disabled Doctors Program—A 5-Year Review," *Journal of the Medical Association of Georgia 70*: 1981, pp. 545-59.

12. J. H. Shore, "The Impaired Physician Four Years After Probation," *Journal of the American Medical Association 248*: December 17, 1982, pp. 3127-30.

13. I. F. Small et al., "The Fate of the Mentally Ill Physician," *American Journal of Psychiatry 125*: 1969, pp. 1333-42.

14. R. M. Murray, "Characteristics and Prognosis of Alcoholic Doctors," *British Medical Journal*, December 25, 1976, pp. 1537-39.

15. M. J. Goby et al., "Physicians Treated for Alcoholism: A Follow-Up Study," *Alcoholism: Clinical and Experimental Research 3*: 1979, pp. 121-24.

16. R. M. Morse et al., "Prognosis of Physicians Treated for Alcoholism and Drug Dependence," *Journal of the American Medical Association 251*: February 10, 1984, pp. 743-746.

17. D. J. Kliner et al., "Treatment Outcome of Alcoholic Physicians," *Journal of Studies on Alcohol 41*: 1980, pp. 1217-20.

18. D. E. Smith, "Substance Abusing Physicians as Patients: Unique Aspects of Treatment," *Conference Proceedings of the California Medical Association*, Committee on the Well-Being of Physicians, San Francisco, 1978, pp. 13-18.

19. "Analysis of the 1980 Survey of the Membership of A.A." (unpublished), New York: Alcoholics Anonymous, 1980.

20. A. Geller, *Alcohol and Anxiety*, Minneapolis, Minn.: Johnson Institute, 1983.

21. *Data from Drug Abuse Warning Network*, Statistical Series I, No. 2, Annual Data 1982, p. 40, Rockville, Md.: National Institute on Drug Abuse, 1983.

TWO

Addressing the Problem

7

The Professional as a Member of A.A.

BASIC ASSUMPTIONS

When a treatment program is described as having an A.A. orientation, this usually means not only that its patients are introduced to A.A. and often guided through the first five steps of the A.A. program, but that certain basic assumptions are accepted as well (1). These include acceptance of alcoholism as a primary disease and one not subject to cure, in the sense that one can expect a safe return to drinking after treatment. Instead, it is seen as a disease whose course can be arrested and can permit a full return to normal functioning if there is no further use of alcohol or other addictive drugs.

The patient is not regarded as responsible for being an alcoholic. The approach of A.A. is that alcoholism, like other illness, happens to people who neither want it, choose it, nor plan to have it. In a sense it is self-inflicted, just as is a hockey player's sprained ankle. The sprain would not have occurred had the player stayed off the ice. Alcoholic behavior would not have occurred had there been no drinking. The player meant to enjoy the game without injury. The alcoholic meant to enjoy drinking and to stop before getting into trouble. By striking judgmental postures and assigning blame we do not help the alcoholic; understanding the nature of alcoholism does. Like it or not, the patient, while not held accountable for becoming alcoholic, is held responsible for cooperating with treatment.

The twelve steps of the A.A. program describe the steps taken by the original members of A.A. and are suggested as actions that others might take since the founders had found them effective. Only the first step mentions alcohol (Appendix B). The steps delineate a process that begins with acceptance that a problem (alcoholism) exists and that, while previous efforts have failed, there is reason for optimism if one relies on God (or on the group alone, if the idea of a personal God is not acceptable). Past mistakes and misdeeds are to be honestly acknowledged and, when feasible, set right. The alcoholic is to become known to at least one other person, a step that counteracts some of the isolation and extreme loneliness so commonly experienced. One then continues a personal inventory so as not to lose awareness of those aspects of the self that, if ignored, can lead to self-deception, problems with self-esteem, tension, discomfort, and then eventually back to the alcohol, which so predictably relieves or changes for a while these unwanted feelings. The goal of these steps is to give the member a sense of comfort with self and others.

This is obviously not done overnight. The expectation is that one will remain an A.A. member, continue to "work the steps," and attend meetings indefinitely. Since it is not regarded as "treatment," there is no expectation that the process should end or be completed at any particular time.

TWELFTH-STEP WORK VERSUS TREATMENT

The last step is the well-known Twelfth Step, the one in which "we try to carry this message" to the alcoholic who still suffers. The A.A. member doing Twelfth-Step work and the professional treating or serving a client are doing quite different things, and the approach of each may well prove alien to the other. There is no exchange of money in Twelfth-Step work. It is understood that this effort is not designed solely to assist the newcomer but is also expected to help the helper maintain sobriety. Since what is to be carried is "the message, not the alcoholic," the A.A. member does not feel responsible for the outcome of the effort. Experience, strength, and hope are to be shared, contacts with other members offered, literature and information given, and invitations to meetings extended. However, it is entirely up to the newcomer to decide what to accept or reject, whether or not to join a group, whether or not to request a sponsor, and even whether or not he or she is alcoholic. Usually Twelfth-Step work is done in pairs and people work with others of the same sex. If a member feels stressed and uncomfortable doing it, he or she can decline formal Twelfth-Step work and the new "pigeon" or "baby" can be passed along to someone else.

No A.A. member is seen as particularly expert; officers rotate and "are but trusted servants." There are no authorities or presidents. The newcomer who wants to pay for help received may well be thanked instead for allowing others the opportunity to help and for the reminder of what active alcoholism is like. The expectation is that the new member will later help someone else in turn, so that there is no need to carry the burden of gratitude.

This approach may seem strange to the professional who expects to seek out and pay for the best treatment. Most of our subjects had never attended an A.A. meeting until compelled to go by their own needs. Most had been taught little or nothing about A.A. in the course of professional training. Many regarded it as a kind of folk medicine and themselves as in particular disgrace since, in spite of all their training, they needed lay help. Bad enough to be alcoholic but worse to be seen at A.A.!

Not only do professionals have trouble understanding A.A.'s way of doing things, but sometimes the fellowship does not do well by them. If the new arrival falls into the category of elite or special persons, the group may forsake what it usually does quite well in order to make unusual and sometimes counterproductive efforts. The prominent judge, the oral surgeon, and the social work director may represent what one A.A. member called "prize pelts," so that there develops an atypical stake in whether or not this particular person stays sober. This can create an unusual kind of pressure and various attempts, literal and figurative, to smell the newcomer's breath or check on attendance at meetings, both maneuvers quite likely to make an ambivalent alcoholic feel resentful and thirsty. In a sincere effort to help, the fellowship may hound instead and, through their own anxiety, risk repeating some of the manipulations and maneuvers already pursued unsuccessfully by the alcoholic's own family. A new arrival at A.A. once asked an old-timer: "How will you know if I stay

sober?" The reply—"I won't, but you will"—was an effortless
return of responsibility to the alcoholic where it belonged. However, this attitude is almost impossible to achieve for someone
deeply invested in a specific outcome. In a small community
the arrival of a prominent citizen truly is an event for the
A.A. group and there is a great deal of interest as well as an
increased chance of gossip. (Even though most of the neighbors
in a small town will turn out to have been aware of the drinking
problem long before the alcoholic was agonizing over being
caught trying to solve it, the realization that people already knew
comes much later, not when it might be useful.)

The "Twelfth Steppers" are at times intimidated by the professional as well and may feel that they have little or nothing of
value to offer someone who must already know all about alcohol,
drugs, and treatment. Even in big cities, professionals who have
initially fretted that A.A. members will find out who they are and
what they do usually lose very little time in seeing to it that the
group *does* learn. Used to flashing their credentials and expecting
deference because of their training, they are uncomfortable doing
without their usual status and rapidly arrange to be discovered.
Tempted into assuming a more familiar role, they tend to play
expert and risk missing out on important parts of the usual A.A.
experience while remaining unaware that this has occurred.

SPECIAL GROUPS

A great many special groups have developed both within and
parallel to A.A. Many are limited to members of particular professions. (See Appendix C.) Most do not attempt to function in
competition with or as substitutes for A.A. Some see themselves as
"vestibule groups," points of entry where fearful newcomers can
meet people like themselves who will, in turn, guide them through
the affiliation process with "outside A.A." Most do not meet
frequently enough to substitute for the regular groups, even if
that were desirable. Of our subjects, 76 percent of the physicians
and 55 percent of the dentists belonged to International Doctors
in A.A. which meets annually in a single weekend. All but 10
were members of regular groups as well.

There was almost full agreement among those who gave an
opinion on this subject that attendance at, and ability to use,
regular A.A. groups was essential. There was also agreement that

contact with a group of colleagues offered something of special value as well. Ideally, they felt there should be both—one system for contact with a variety of people outside the confines of one's professional world, but also, when possible, the chance to share those particular concerns and questions common to one's own discipline that outsiders never live and experience. Some said that they would never have approached A.A. had they not been put in touch with another judge or a fellow surgeon. Others, particularly the women, felt that the important thing was just to know an acceptable woman who "had been there"; what she did for a career was of little importance. One said that she would have chosen almost anyone rather than another nurse, that her greatest fear was the reaction of others in her profession if they knew.

Available groups and personal preferences have varied and will continue to do so. The only certainty is that many more groups and many more kinds of A.A. groups exist than anyone of us knows. There is no agency, not even A.A.'s General Service Office, that has a complete list of groups, and changes are so rapid that any such catalog would be obsolete almost at once. A determined search for even a highly unlikely group may well result in finding that one of the desired makeup does exist.

THE RECOVERED PROFESSIONAL AS A TREATER OF OTHER ALCOHOLICS

Many recovered alcoholics regardless of background decide to make a new career as a counselor. Most of the older and more experienced alcoholism treatment centers will not hire a "recovered" alcoholic with less than two to three years of "clean and dry" health plus "good quality" sobriety, stable A.A. membership, and evidence of ability to function successfully in some field of employment unrelated to his or her personal health history (2,3). In addition, the would-be counselor is expected to acquire appropriate training to fulfill this new role and to work toward gaining credentials as a Certified Alcoholism Counselor (C.A.C.). As one excellent counselor put it, "Just because you had your appendix out doesn't fit you to take out mine. It may get you interested, but that's all!"

When an applicant's only credential for working in the field is his or her personal alcoholic or drug experience, it is usually fairly easy to persuade the person that, if the career change is right, it will still be right in a year or two and that, initially, additional Twelfth-Step experience, some training courses, and perhaps A.A. volunteer work in institutions like jails and hospitals will provide valuable interim experience. One can only urge the aspiring counselor to make haste slowly while his or her own recovery is consolidated—before the stress of role change to counselor occurs, with the inevitable distancing of self from the distress of others, and before tackling the dilemmas that follow when today's patients appear as members of one's own A.A. group tonight.

However, there is no easy way to put brakes on the impatient professional. Those with degrees in psychiatric nursing, for example, or social work are already treating people for a living. They rapidly discover that quite a few of their existing patients are alcoholics. In addition, members of local A.A. groups may be delighted to have one of their own to whom they can refer. Since treatment facilities were for many years short of good quality staff willing to work with alcoholics, they held out an array of tempting offers. It was easy to rationalize that, prepared or not, one was needed and the rush to rescue began. All too often there was little or no perception that there was a body of knowledge to be mastered and, lacking that awareness, no attempt was made to acquire it. Physicians in particular were likely to become alcohol program director with little or no background for the job. When simply diagnosing, detoxicating, and introducing a patient to A.A. did not always work, failure could be blamed on the patient. Not only has this at times led to poor patient care, but it has increased pressure on the treater, a situation which all too often is followed by a relapse.

To be truly knowledgeable about alcoholism treatment and to bring to it the special empathy of someone with personal experience of the illness, and how it affects the self and family, can permit many professionals to make exceptional contributions. To do this well requires a great deal of self-knowledge and self-awareness, so that the old patterns that are less healthy can be understood and avoided rather than perhaps reinforced in people with the same problem. This too is not an overnight achievement.

Unlike the layperson, the professional often has the power to get into a position of authority very quickly, whether or not there has been good preparation. The result obviously can be very good or very bad. Interestingly, some of the most dramatic examples at both extremes have been physician husbands of alcoholics who, after the wife's recovery, make a career of managing alcoholism in others. (It was not infrequent that we learned of physician husbands who not only had treated their wives for years but had used huge amounts of drugs, including injectable narcotics, in the process.)

ANONYMITY

Just as professionals can bypass the usual preparation for treating others, they frequently go through a period of finding fault with A.A., wanting to reorganize it and expressing impatience that it will not recruit more aggressively. Some individual physicians decide that the rules that apply to laypersons do not apply to them and proceed to ignore A.A.'s request that they not identify themselves as A.A. members at the media level. (A.A.'s anonymity tradition is designed not only to reassure the newcomer that the group will keep a confidence, but to avoid having self-appointed spokespersons interpreting A.A. policy according to personal whim and to avoid the dangers of self-aggrandizement for the attention seeker.)

Members are free to tell anyone they like that they belong to A.A. if media are not involved so long as they do not break the anonymity of any others without specific permission of the individual involved. Some are content with telling their personal experience in journal articles, but others, almost always physicians, have gone to the extreme of collecting and disseminating names of fellow A.A. physicians for a variety of purposes. Although their motives may have been pure enough, in certain situations a physician had less anonymity than an ordinary newcomer and a fellow physician was actually causing the problem! Particularly now with malpractice suits on the rise and generous statutes of limitations, professionals with a practice and clients will need confidentiality to help them get on their feet.

Many of the problems as well as the legitimate complaints of professionals and others that more needs to be done for alcoholics than A.A. now attempts to do can be addressed through other organizations (see Chapter 8 and Appendix C) distinct from A.A. and not restricted by its traditions. For example, at its annual steering committee meeting, International Doctors in A.A. has to deal with innumerable requests that it operate a job bank, rent its membership list to marketers of books, vitamins, and continuing education courses, or undertake the education of medical students. These projects are usually acknowledged as having merit but not being within the purview of an A.A. group and they are gently but firmly declined; those seeking help are redirected to other agencies, such as the American Medical Society on Alcoholism.

SPECIAL OPPORTUNITY

Just as a professional may have some unique problems in working out a comfortable accommodation with an A.A. group, there is also the possibility of an unusual chance to be of service. As alcoholism treatment facilities have appeared literally by the hundreds in recent years, they have directed a flood of newly discharged patients, professional and layperson alike, to A.A. groups whose volunteers may or may not be equipped to handle the volume. There have been the inevitable problems of communication and misunderstanding of each other's expectations as both referring professionals and A.A. members struggle with their own preconceptions and misconceptions of one another.

The professional who is familiar with and belongs to both worlds—that of A.A. and that of the profession as well—can be of enormous value in interpreting each group's motives to the other. Nurses, social workers, and attorneys do what they do for a reason and in a context that often seems quite arbitrary to an outsider. A.A. in turn has developed its own behaviors and traditions pragmatically through years of experience with what works and what does not (4). Once securely sober and having thought through the timing and the other considerations of who is to know what, the person who wears two hats can help bridge the gap between his or her colleagues and A.A., and often in the process can understand more fully and resolve some of the same discomforts he or she is experiencing.

PARTICIPATION IN A.A.

As described in Chapter 5, most of our subjects found that anticipated problems with religiosity or socioeconomic status with regard to A.A. ideals and membership were not as great as subjects had feared. We also found that newly sober members tended to go to A.A. meetings more often than those with longer periods of abstinence. While the subjects themselves were often apologetic for infrequent attendance and wanted to reassure their interviewer that they were not minimizing the risk of relapse (or perhaps not to appear disloyal to A.A.), some professionals who were not members were critical of A.A. members who were regular attenders. Regular attendance at A.A. was interpreted as one symptom of dependency having been substituted for another. Other critics have worried that the A.A. subculture might create a self-imposed ghetto that would isolate and limit.

We were curious to know if, with longer sobriety, A.A. attendance would continue to decrease for a group studied prospectively. We asked about the usual rate of A.A. attendance as well as the actual number of meetings attended in the 30 days preceding each interview. In our group of subjects, 12 percent had not attended at all in the month prior to the second interview, while only 4 percent had failed to attend in the month prior to the first interview. The number attending every two weeks or more remained quite constant: 72 percent on first interview and 71 percent on the second. Since so few had resumed drinking, one cannot explain this by postulating that after relapse they had resumed a beginner's frequent attendance pattern. It is more likely that, since the median length of sobriety for the entire group was already six years at initial interview, this particular group had settled on a somewhat static pattern of behavior.

SOCIAL LIFE

The issue of social life and chosen circle of friends became more complex as we listened to interviews. Patterns emerged as faint outlines, later as hypotheses to be explored. If there was a new marriage to an A.A. member, the couple often spent a great deal of time with their fellow A.A. members. If there was a spouse not in Al-Anon who continued to drink, less time was spent with A.A. people, and the couple either lived part-time in both the drinking and nondrinking world or the alcoholic would go to A.A. meetings but limit A.A. contact to that. (This second pattern was often mentioned when the wife was the alcoholic, as if the husband's was the more important world from which she would foray for business only.) In very small communities with few available meetings and few choices among the few members, less time was spent with other A.A. members than in the cities where almost any kind of person can be found within the fellowship.

There was very little difference over time in the subjects' reported estimates of what percentage of their social activities is spent with other A.A. members. At first interview there were 35 percent and at follow-up 43 percent who reported spending two-fifths or less of their time with other A.A. members. Thus, about the same time was spent with other A.A. members after more years of sobriety; we did not see any obvious pattern of moving to other circles. There was little sense that subjects felt any pressure either to seek safety within the fellowship or to "outgrow it." Most who volunteered an explanation said that being with heavy drinkers did not upset them and that those drinkers were perceived as boring rather than threatening. Others noted that some of their old friends who were former heavy drinking companions had died or had become A.A. members themselves.

When our subjects were asked if they served alcohol in their homes, the initial interview and follow-up proportions were similar. At initial interview, 73 percent served alcohol in their homes and, at follow-up, 74 percent did so. When asked if they would drink again if they could do so safely, there was little change. Twenty-six percent would have done so when first interviewed; 23 percent still would, when asked again.

SELF-DISCLOSURE

When first interviewed almost all subjects were known by their families to be A.A. members, and 81 percent were known by most colleagues and co-workers to be members—proportions that did not change to any significant degree between the two interviews. Perhaps a few more colleagues or a few more close friends were told or learned of it in time. Several more licensing boards knew, probably as individuals revealed their own recovery in the process of working out systems to help others. The only dramatic difference in level of anonymity between interviews was in the impression that subjects had about their image in the community. While initially exactly 55 percent of both men and women felt the general public in their communities was aware of their A.A.

membership, by follow-up this had jumped to 87 percent of the men and 90 percent of the women.

Subjects stated repeatedly that time had removed most of the anxiety about exposure, that the major upsets and embarrassments were in the past, and that these things were unlikely to pose a threat no matter who might learn of them now. In addition, there were often expressions of much greater acceptance of self as someone who had been ill and recovered from a legitimate ailment rather than someone who had been bad and subsequently reformed. (A.A. members detest the term "reformed alcoholic" with its moralistic overtones, since one does not reform from diabetes, hypothyroidism, or other nonstigmatized diseases.) Apparently our subjects became more comfortable with themselves, more secure in their length of recovery, and, in most cases, continued their fellowship with A.A.; thus there was little remaining concern that others would find out, and most of their friends had in fact been told.

For most in our study group, anonymity was of little importance in day-to-day living. However, the newcomer making a first tentative approach to an A.A. member or group will continue to need the assurance that the tradition will remain and that self-disclosure is a personal choice, and no one else's.

INTERNATIONAL DOCTORS IN A.A.

The professions we have studied, as well as other occupational groups, have created their own support groups—sometimes entirely within an A.A. framework, sometimes not, and sometimes forming simultaneous but different groups in order to serve different functions. (See Appendix C for a listing of groups and contacts, and Chapters 8 and 9.) The oldest and largest of the A.A. groups for professionals, International Doctors in A.A. (IDAA), first met in 1949 in Cape Vincent, New York, when Clarence P., a physician in general practice, placed a notice in the A.A. Grapevine (a newsletter) inviting any other recovered doctors and their wives to his home (5). Appreciative of A.A., but feeling isolated without the presence of another physician, he was eager to know if there were others and if they too missed the shop talk, camaraderie, and reassurance of peers. Some 20 doctors of medicine, dentistry, and psychology from the United States and Canada converged on his hastily improvised garage meeting room, one psychiatrist driving all the way from Denver!

Except for a year's hiatus in 1950, this group has met annually ever since, usually for an early August weekend. Its mailing list numbers well over 2,500 and its meetings, which are held in different sites in the United States and Canada, now draw 300 to 500 members. Doctoral-level people in all fields of health care and the medical sciences are welcome, as are matriculated students still earning their degrees. Medical students and house staff, once a rarity, are now almost commonplace at these meetings. Couples are also welcome, regardless of whether the alcoholism has been present in the doctor or in the spouse.

These annual meetings have increased in length as well as in the number of attendees they draw. Frequently, they now include a separate, scientific session for continuing education credits, which can help with tax advantages. Although one hears references to "IDAA chapters," IDAA is not an umbrella organization and does not actually have chapters, although there are now many similar local and regional groups of professionals operating under a variety of different names, membership requirements, and ground rules. The secretary of the organization does try, however, to keep abreast of where most of these groups are located, both in the United States and abroad.

IDAA sees itself as very much an A.A. group even though it does restrict membership. It receives frequent requests to take on a variety of other non-A.A. activities, such as running a job bank, monitoring or attesting to a doctor's amount or quality of sobriety, endorsing particular treatment modalities or settings, or backing the position of an individual medical educator or politician. The group has wisely avoided most of these other agendas in favor of providing a support network to individuals and an opportunity for its members to come together and address more personal needs. Between meetings it arranges contacts between individuals and helps new members locate other recovered professionals. Members are, of course, entirely free to involve themselves in the broader field of alcoholism as individuals, and a great many have done so through organizations like the 1,400-member American Medical Society on Alcoholism, which includes physicians interested in alcoholism and in addiction to other psychotropic drugs as well.

Since dentists, osteopathic physicians, veterinarians, and psychologists have been full members of IDAA from the outset, they have not yet indicated a need to form any additional national A.A. group for doctors.

THE BRITISH DOCTORS GROUP

The London group began in 1973 when two general practitioners began to meet regularly to discuss problems in their recovery from alcoholism. Some months later a few alcoholic doctors known to them were invited to join the group, continued to attend regularly, and proved willing to travel long distances in order to do so, some coming from the north of England. The London group continues to hold a monthly Saturday meeting in a centrally located hotel, which includes a three-hour discussion of varying content, followed by a meal.

In its last five years the group has had over 200 contacts in Great Britain (6). The group also somewhat informally coordinates a total of seven different groups in Ireland and Great Britain. Most of the members use the A.A. fellowship as well as the British Doctors Group, but a few do not. The meetings are private and confidential and are limited to helping doctors and dentists. At times, invitations are extended to nonalcoholic colleagues in order to maintain a liaison between the group and directors of alcoholic treatment centers both in the National Health Service and the private sector. The group is independent and not affiliated with any other organization, although it works with the Medical Defence Union and the Medical Protection Society. In cases where the General Medical Council has instigated proceedings against alcoholic doctors, members have given evidence before the council attesting to the efforts or lack of effort made by a doctor in maintaining sobriety. Group members are available on request to visit other alcoholic doctors at home or in the hospital.

The British Doctors Group has been quite aggressive in making its presence known both through lay and medical media (7,8), while IDAA has acted more strictly according to the A.A. tradition of public relations based on "attraction, not promotion." Although the British Doctors Group makes a concerted effort to steer its members into A.A., it is not officially an A.A. group. It concurs with IDAA's approach to alcoholism:

> Like our colleagues in the U.S.A., we are firmly committed to total abstinence . . . from alcohol and all mood-changing drugs, also believing that this must be the primary goal for treatment. . . . As a group we have yet to learn of a single case of a successful return to "controlled" drinking. All such attempts have sooner or later ended in failure. Sadly, some of our members have died still believing they could control their drinking and four have committed suicide.

For three years the British Doctors Group has held successful annual conventions, near London, in Durham, and in the Lake District. It has recently initiated regular meetings for family members in London and the North-East area. The group is self-supporting from contributions collected at meetings and from an annual appeal to members. It began the same year (1973) the *Journal of the American Medical Association* (JAMA) published the landmark article entitled "The Sick Physician" by Rogers Smith (9); it preceded by two years the Merrison report, which acknowledged that England and the United States were both facing similar difficulties, stating in so many words: "There's a sick doctor problem and the existing NHS controls cannot cope with it" (10).

INTERNATIONAL LAWYERS IN A.A.

International Lawyers in A.A. (ILAA) is closely patterned on IDAA and operates in a very similar fashion. Founded in 1975 (11), it is much newer and therefore considerably smaller. While it is growing very steadily and its membership already exceeds 600, it competes for attention with the other, sometimes very vigorous, advocacy efforts within the legal profession such as Lawyers Concerned for Lawyers (LCL). (See Chapter 10 and Appendix C.)

ENGLISH ALCOHOLIC GROUP FOR LAWYERS

Just organized is the English Alcoholic Group for Lawyers (EAGL). Its membership is open to any lawyer, practicing or not, whether barrister, solicitor, judge, or those of "paralegal" status, such as the legal, executive clerk or unadmitted clerk. They describe themselves as

> an informal group of lawyers in Britain who are recovering alcoholics and who are willing to make ourselves available in complete confidence to lawyers who need help with a drinking problem or cross-addiction to other drugs, whether called upon personally or by concerned partners, colleagues or families. We are self-supporting and independent; our experience is that alcoholism is a recognizable and treatable condition from which recovery is possible with help.

GROUPS FOR NURSES AND SOCIAL WORKERS

There are many local groups of nurses, some following an A.A. format and others modifying it. Quite recently, the National Nurses Society on Addictions has begun collecting information for a directory of these and other support groups. There is no national group specifically for recovered nurses. Social Workers Helping Social Workers, while not an A.A. group, is largely composed of A.A. members and, like the British Doctors Group, can offer personal contacts and networking (Appendix C).

OTHER GROUPS FOR THE HELPING PROFESSIONS

In addition to those named above, several other versions of A.A. groups exist, such as Caduceus in New York City, which accepts a variety of health-care professionals including nurses, physicians, and social workers, and stag groups, including one limited to male physicians and Catholic priests and another for male physicians and male nurses. A.A. as an organization prefers that any group that restricts its membership call itself a "meeting" rather than a "group," since traditionally the fellowship believes that all A.A. groups should welcome all alcoholics. Special-interest meetings are, as previously noted, quite common and include, among many others, Birds of a Feather (airline pilots), Flying High and The Doves (flight attendants), Internationalists (merchant seamen), and Cops and Robbers (police and ex-convicts). Meetings are also conducted in American sign language for the deaf, and some cater primarily to various other groups: women, young people, gay men and lesbians, those who have been dually addicted (alcohol and drugs), or those who have relapsed after prolonged sobriety and are having trouble coming back. A.A. members are free to belong to as few or as many groups as they choose and to attend as often or as rarely as they wish.

Some A.A. members are highly disapproving of any special groups whatsoever, but most seem perfectly willing to accept whatever pique they may feel at being excluded from certain meetings if the existence of the special group enables another alcoholic to survive who otherwise might not. So long as the special group is seen as a supplement to, rather than as a substitute for, the broader A.A. experience, there seems to be a consensus that the pluses far outweigh the possible hazards. Only when motivation for these groups is seen as snobbery or elitism for its own sake is there a problem.

REFERENCES

1. N. G. Hoffman et al., "Alcoholics Anonymous after Treatment: Attendance and Abstinence," *International Journal of the Addictions 18*: 1983, pp. 311–18.

2. L. Bissell, "Recovered Alcoholic Counselors," in: *Encyclopedic Handbook of Alcoholism*, E. M. Pattison and E. Kaufman, eds., New York: Gardner Press, 1982, pp. 810–17.

3. B. L. King et al., "Alcoholics Anonymous, Alcoholism Counseling, and Social Work Treatment," *Health and Social Work 4*: April 1979, pp. 182–98.

4. *Twelve Steps and Twelve Traditions*, New York: Alcoholics Anonymous World Services, Inc., 1953.

5. "Doctors in A.A.," *A.A. Grapevine 18*: January 1962, pp. 16–19.

6. British Doctors Group, "Doctors and the Bottle," London: *The Medical Council on Alcoholism*, Spring 1983.

7. "British Doctors Group: The First Five Years," *British Journal on Alcohol and Alcoholism 15*: 1980, pp. 13–16.

8. J. Charles, "Alcoholism, Hitting the Bottle," *General Practitioner* (London), February 11, 1969.

9. American Medical Association, Council on Mental Health, "The Sick Physician," *Journal of the American Medical Association 223*: February 5, 1973, pp. 684–87.

10. A. W. Merrison, *Report of the Committee of Inquiry into the Regulation of the Medical Profession*, London: Her Majesty's Stationery Office, April 1975.

11. "International Lawyers in A.A.," *A.A. Grapevine 34*: September 1977, pp. 18–19.

8

The Organizational Response of Professions in Our Study

As interest in impaired professionals has grown in the last few years and the status of the subject has moved from unmentionable to almost stylish, many "experts" and schemes for intervention or even prevention have appeared. There is still a great deal of concealment designed to protect a colleague's reputation or to avoid jeopardizing third-party payment for treatment. This remains true even though the stigma of being an alcoholic is not as great as it once was and subterfuge on the part of colleagues may be less common.

Of nearly 800 physicians responding to an anonymous questionnaire distributed at a Continuing Medical Education course which is given annually at the Mayo Clinic, most agreed that impaired physicians should be evaluated and treated (1). At the same time, these doctors were extremely reluctant to participate in the reporting process. Many would do nothing to intervene unless a colleague's ability to practice was seriously impaired and some, even then, would do nothing. While the more cynical suggest that the profession is more interested in avoiding lawsuits than in patient care, a growing awareness of effective treatment techniques is probably more important in fostering change.

The first profession to acknowledge and address the alcoholism of its members appears to have been the Roman Catholic Church, which for many years has offered residential treatment to alcoholic priests in facilities like Guest House in Lake Orion, Michigan, and, more recently, Marsalin Institute in Holliston, Massachusetts, where women in religious orders were accepted as well.

ORGANIZED MEDICINE—
THE AMERICAN MEDICAL ASSOCIATION
AND STATE MEDICAL SOCIETIES

Organized medicine was next to follow. Concern among physicians for their alcoholic or addicted peers was not new. Groups such as the Friends of Medicine in the Pacific Northwest and New York's Physicians' Home for years have tried to help physicians with a variety of problems. It is probably not accidental that the recovery of many physicians in A.A. was followed by the development of a host of programs to offer assistance to those still in trouble. Almost one-third of the 481 members of impaired physician committees who were a part of a 1980 study by the American Medical Association (AMA) were former addicts or recovered alcoholics (2). As improved treatment gave increasing reason for optimism, the energy and sometimes almost evangelical enthusiasm of the recovered alcoholic merged with the efforts of the many who had already been urging that something more be done.

In 1973, the AMA's Council of Mental Health issued its landmark report on "The Sick Physician." It acknowledged "a physician's ethical responsibility to take cognizance of a colleague's inability to practice medicine adequately by reason of physical or mental illness, including alcoholism or drug dependence" and goes on to assert that, when the exhortations of friends and family fail and the physician cannot make a rational assessment of his or her ability to function professionally, "it becomes essentially the responsibility of his colleagues to make that assessment for him and to advise him whether he should obtain treatment and curtail or suspend his practice" (3). This was later formalized as AMA policy by approval of the House of Delegates.

To make it possible to intervene when a physician was unlikely to be able to practice "with reasonable skill and safety" but without having to wait until a patient was actively harmed, the AMA's legislative department designed and made available a model law (4). First enacted in Florida, various sick physician statutes, many based on the AMA model, had by 1980 been enacted by nearly 40 states. At present, all 50 states have in place, or at least are in the process of forming, some type of impaired physician committee. Since 1975, the AMA has sponsored national conferences at roughly two-year intervals to address the subject. These have attracted hundreds of concerned physicians and have provided an opportunity for the sharing of problems and intervention techniques. [The first such conference considered the "disabled" physician, but this term was already in use by other doctors with physical disabilities. Since the word "impaired" was both neutral and unclaimed, it was adopted instead.]

Individual state efforts vary greatly in quality, in level of activity, and in ability to help. Some are still very new, tentative, and inexperienced. Others remain handicapped by archaic state laws. Some do an excellent job of outreach and referral to effective treatment. Some are essentially paralyzed by their own timidity. Still others are entirely too casual about the individual physician's right to due process and to privacy.

Approaches to the problems of self-regulation differ widely, and the way in which the alcoholic is approached is inevitably part of this larger picture. While some states provide for intervention before a sick or impaired doctor has done any harm, others still require proof that a law has been broken or that damage has occurred. In some states, the medical profession itself has much of the power to grant, revoke, or suspend a license to practice. In others, this authority is held entirely by one or more government agencies; thus in these cases physicians cannot regulate each other's behavior. Where the AMA model law has been enacted, more flexibility and greater effectiveness are possible.

The Canadian Medical Association has made no formal alcoholism policy statements nor offered specific direction to the provinces, some of which do have quite active intervention programs of their own.

OSTEOPATHIC MEDICINE

The American Osteopathic Association (AOA) resolved in 1973 (and reaffirmed its intent again in 1978) to establish a committee to study the feasibility of establishing permanent committees in its divisional societies to assist in the rehabilitation of impaired osteopathic physicians (5). Specifically, the committees would address those whose incapacity resulted from psychiatric disorders, alcoholism, drug dependence, and other incapacitating physical problems. A very few such committees do exist, although the AOA does not at present have available a listing of them. They seem to have been formed independently of any national effort and on a state rather than on a regional basis. Contact among them has been entirely informal. Texas appears to have the oldest and most solidly established committee (Appendix C); Arizona, the newest.

There are far fewer osteopaths than medical doctors, and osteopaths seem to be concentrated in relatively few states. Frequently, they have solo practices in small communities and rural areas rather than in the social groups and organizational hierarchies where alcohol problems are more likely to be seen by colleagues and those in authority.

A number of osteopathic physicians attend the AMA Impaired Physician conferences, and individuals do work informally with the allopathic state-level committees. Other individuals are active members of International Doctors in A.A. and the American Medical Society on Alcoholism. While the initial forthright acknowledgment of the alcohol problem in the profession was almost simultaneous by both the AMA and AOA, the latter group apparently has not yet been able to translate its original statement of intent into specific recommendations for local action.

SOCIETIES IN THE MEDICAL PROFESSION

American Psychiatric Association

Several societies within the medical profession, aware that they may learn of an impaired specialist sooner than a state program, have also taken an interest in helping impaired colleagues. The American Psychiatric Association's Task Force on the Impaired Physician (renamed the Committee on the Impaired Physician in 1980) was formed in 1979. It has worked to obtain psychiatric services for medical students, to develop standards of confidentiality concerning a physician's mental health, and to establish guidelines for the district branches to work with the existing impaired physician programs of the state medical societies. It has preferred to urge collaboration rather than the establishment of a parallel and competing system, although several branches do have their own committees. The guidelines suggest educational programs, work with spouses, and help with reentry into the profession. Alcoholism has not been singled out for special attention and remains under the rubric of impairment in general (6).

American Academy of Family Practice

The American Academy of Family Practice (AAFP) has a Committee on Mental Health that views physician impairment, including that caused by alcoholism, "as any other disease." It sees its role primarily as educational and as a builder of support systems. It has taken a great interest in the physician living alone, who is perhaps particularly vulnerable to dangerous ways of coping (7).

American College of Obstetricians and Gynecologists

The Executive Board of the American College of Obstetricians and Gynecologists (ACOG) approved a policy statement on the impaired physician in 1980 and urged its sections to cooperate with state medical society committees. Members are encouraged to help with the further development of state programs and to assist in sharing information, in confronting the impaired physician (who may be a fellow of the College), and in arranging coverage for that individual's practice (8).

American Occupational Medical Association

According to Fern Asma, a medical doctor formerly active in Illinois Bell's pioneer employee assistance program (9), this 4,000-member specialty group includes many American and Canadian physicians who do not belong to other medical organizations and who frequently have little contact with many other doctors. The program she is designing for them hopes to provide better case-finding methods and intervention for members who are likely to escape attention in the existing systems. Her Committee to Aid Impaired Physicians has already been involved with several cases. The American Occupational Medical Association (AOMA) would prefer to tie in with existing state committees rather than duplicate their efforts. It agrees that coercion into treatment may at times be necessary. Just as their personal familiarity with the law makes intervention models devised by attorneys of particular interest to those concerned with due process and risk of litigation, AOMA methods, though still embryonic, will be worth watching as well. These are the men and women who have for many years provided input and supervision to industrial Employee Assistance Programs (EAPs), most of which in the major corporations are based in either the medical or personnel departments. If ways are found to maximize this special background and if it can then be combined with members' understanding of their fellow physicians, their final procedures will be particularly worth studying.

American Medical Society on Alcoholism

The American Medical Society on Alcoholism (AMSA) was founded in 1954 as the New York City Medical Society on Alcoholism. In 1967, it became a national society and now represents over 1,400 physicians of many disciplines with a common interest in alcohol and other drugs of addiction. It works in collaboration with the National Council on Alcoholism but is entirely separate from it. It has developed many statements concerning alcoholism and alcohol use, including criteria for the diagnosis of alcoholism (10) and a definition of recovery from it. Its members were very active in developing the state-level impaired physicians committees, have been prominent in the five AMA-sponsored national conferences, and have frequently participated in "horrible example" panels, a teaching effort in which alcoholic and addicted physicians who have recovered successfully describe their personal experience for medical students. These exercises in the personal and human aspects of the disease rather than in the intellectual and theoretical are said to be of great interest to the students.

AMSA does have a committee on the impaired physician but it has not yet felt the need to make statements about alcoholism in professionals as distinct from other patients. The committee's most recent concern has been with individual physicians, some of them AMSA members, who are experiencing drinking problems. Many state-level committees are either too new or still not yet forceful enough to manage some of their very senior, very prominent, and very powerful colleagues. Since these alcoholic men and women themselves may be highly visible experts in the field of alcoholism and addiction, their special position and special knowledge is at times used to intimidate others as well as to reinforce their own denial of a problem. (See Appendix C, under AMSA.) Compounding the resistance to self-appraisal so common in alcoholic physicians, the expertise of this group makes the denial even more difficult to overcome.

ORGANIZED DENTISTRY

Of the nearly 130,000 professionally active dentists in the United States, about 9,000 "could be alcoholics" according to an article in the November 1982 issue of the *Journal of the American Dental Association* (11). The writer is quick to admit that specific data on alcoholism and other drug use are nonexistent and that, although there is good reason to suspect that dentists are the single group most prone to self-administering nitrous oxide, even that has been little studied.

In 1979, the House of Delegates for the American Dental Association (ADA) asked that the Council on Dental Practice act as a clearinghouse for information on alcoholism and other chemical dependency programs for the dental profession. Dr. John Clarno, himself a dentist and a recovered alcoholic, who has worked as an employee assistance program director since his retirement from dental practice in 1969, was engaged as consultant. (See Appendix C.)

In 1982, the ADA developed and disseminated model legislation to dental societies for assisting impaired dentists. Currently, about 20 state dental societies and half a dozen component societies have established programs to help alcoholic and addicted dentists into treatment.

Late in 1978, Dentists Concerned for Dentists (DCD) was established in Minnesota. Modeled on Lawyers Concerned for Lawyers (LCL), it was composed of recovered alcoholic and chemically dependent dentists. (A similar group, Physicians Serving Physicians, later followed in the early 1980s but did not, for obvious reasons, select similar initials.) DCD receives both moral and financial backing from the Minnesota Dental Association and, while it does not have out-of-state branches, does serve as a model for similar efforts elsewhere in the country, making available written descriptions of its methods. (See Chapter 10 and Appendix C.)

In July 1982, Herbert Hedge reported on the results of a survey of 35 responding dentists to whom he mailed a questionnaire in 1980 (12). He sent 200 copies of the questionnaire to A.A. groups known to have dentists as members, but we do not know why the response rate was so low. Of the 35 respondents, 18 reported addiction to alcohol, 2 to other drugs, another 15 primarily to alcohol, but with other drugs used as well, and 4 reported habitual use of nitrous oxide. One-third reported addiction prior to dental school and 4 more before it ended. Fifteen (42%) reported addiction in a parent. As in the present study, these respondents stood high in their dental school class at the time of graduation. (It is of course quite possible that some of these same people were subjects in our study as well.) With the exception of the examples cited above and the occasional inclusion of a few individuals described when in treatment with other medical professionals (13), most of the writings about alcoholic dentists are either first-person anecdotes (14,15) or descriptions of individual state efforts reported in their state association journals (16,17,18). There have, however, been quite a number of these accounts in recent years, so that rather than ignoring the problem dentistry has increasingly called attention to it.

One of the career teachers in alcoholism and addiction is Mark S. Arthur, D.D.S., who is part of a federally subsidized cadre of medical school faculty charged with curriculum development in this field. He is an assistant professor of pharmacology, the director of Addictions Education, Alcohol and Drug Abuse at the University of Maryland Dental School, and also the chairman of the Maryland State Dental Association Committee for the Rehabilitation of Dentists.

NURSING

In March of 1978, over 100 nurses from several states gathered in Manhattan for a day-long meeting to discuss the long-neglected problem of the alcoholic nurse (19,20). By 1980, there were also two active organizations of nurses interested in alcoholism and addiction. The Drug and Alcohol Nursing Association (DANA) and National Nurses Society on Addiction (NNSA) both were quick to point out the need for impaired nurse programs. (NNSA maintains a list of resource people in many states who can give information and provide contacts for nurses needing help and of available support groups. Also see Appendix C.) Both nursing groups have been represented on the American Nursing Association's (ANA's) 1981 Nursing Task Force on Addiction and Psychological Disturbance, created in part to formulate guidelines for state nurse associations developing programs to help nurses whose practice is impaired by alcoholism, other drug use, or psychological dysfunction.

In 1982, the ANA House of Delegates adopted a resolution recognizing as part of its responsibility to colleagues and patients the need for timely and effective intervention both for the health of the nurse and for maintenance of nursing practice standards. Employers of alcoholic nurses are urged to offer "appropriate treatment antecedent to disciplinary action in the same manner as with other health problems." Supporters of the resolution had been highly visible at the annual ANA conference with their "Help, don't Hide!" plastic badges. Guidelines for procedures and data collection are urged as well (21).

In April of 1982, the *American Journal of Nursing* published a set of articles called "Help for the Helper" (22), addressing the impaired nurse issue and reporting that four state programs were in place and that three more were being planned. As of Fall 1983, some 25 states had or soon hoped to have such programs. Rapid action to remedy past neglect is taking place. Maryland was the first actually to begin work in this area and started offering its services in early 1980. Within 18 months, its Committee for the Rehabilitation of Impaired Nurses (CRIN) had contact with 57 nurses—27 with alcohol problems, 23 with other drug problems, 2 with psychiatric problems, and 5 with "other functional impairment." Ohio's Peer Assistance Program for Nurses (PAPN) also got started in 1980.

Prior to the 1980s, the problem of narcotic addiction in nursing served as a lightning rod to attract attention away from alcoholism. Even today, when discussing the nurses' use of alcohol and other drugs, the conversation will invariably shift away from the use of alcohol, other sedatives, or stimulants and concentrate on opiate use instead. Addicts have been reported to agents of the law and to state boards. Alcoholics have been urged to resign or be dismissed. A recent JAMA article on drug problems within the field of anesthesiology gives a fine illustration of differential treatment of physicians and registered nurses in its statement that, while some follow-up information is available for the physicians who were helped into treatment, it is not available for the nurses because they were simply fired (23,24).

Nursing has taken narcotic violations very seriously and has agreed to, and cooperated with, the imposition of procedures on nurses that would not readily be accepted by physicians for themselves or their fellows. Even now, a nurse accused of diverting narcotics may be arrested at the hospital where she works, handcuffed, and led off by police in full view of her colleagues. Charges against her, while still unproven, may be given to the press. If her license is lost, quite arbitrary periods of time may be mandated before its return can be considered and the conditions for its restoration may be extremely vague. It is not unusual for a nurse to attend a long-awaited and brief hearing in which she attempts to show as best she can that she has rehabilitated herself only to be told that her efforts are not adequate, yet at the same time she may be given no sound advice as to what she must do in order to satisfy. No clear list of requirements is offered.

After listening to many individual nurses' accounts of their experience with alcoholism, other addictions, and recovery, it seems fair to say that the profession will nurture and protect the alcoholic nurse for long periods, deny the diagnosis or miss it altogether, conceal it, fire if need be, but be very slow in giving her a bad reference or to report her to a board. One nurse who turned herself in for help and who voluntarily surrendered her license as she went into residential treatment has remained entirely drug and alcohol free for nearly three years and has not experienced a relapse. She has completed a master's degree program in nursing, but has yet to have her license restored, nor has she been given clear information about exactly what she must do to regain it. Another nurse in a different state did succeed in regaining her license but had great difficulty in finding work after her previous employer telephoned every other hospital and nursing home in the small city where she lived to ward off other potential employers. Many other nurses have been forced to hire attorneys in order to force reinstatement.

Once a report is filed, former protectors can become a lynch mob, particularly when narcotics are also involved. Unfortunately, when the nurse has been driven from practice and her license is lost, it is extremely difficult for her to regain it.

Since authority has been so reluctant to act—and, when it does, so often to overreact—it is no surprise that nurses hesitate to draw attention to their drinking problems. A classic case involved a doctoral-level nurse on an Ivy League nursing school faculty who was fired as soon as she was discovered to have admitted herself for residential alcoholism treatment. As the profession strengthens its resolve that no nurse be deprived of her career because of an illness, nurses are becoming more insistent on early case-finding methods and on treatment rather than dismissal. An ever-increasing number of nurses have recovered from alcoholism, talk freely of what they experienced, and are active in forming advocacy and support groups such as those listed with NNSA. They urge early recognition and treatment, and that other nurses no longer be forced out of the profession or into early retirement, which is so likely to lead to depression, suicide, and early death. They hope that most alcoholic nurses will continue to remain unknown to state boards, but that this time that will be because the cases are being well managed rather than hidden.

In 1983, Florida amended its laws so that a nurse or physician entering and cooperating with alcoholism treatment need no longer be reported to the state under the "snitch law." If the professional remains defiant, refuses treatment, or will not take it seriously, so that patients are in danger, reporting still can and is expected to occur.

THE LEGAL PROFESSION

While the American Bar Association (ABA) together with the American Medical Association issued a joint statement in 1968 recognizing alcoholism as an illness rather than a moral failing, the ABA has yet to make any statement of policy concerning alcoholic lawyers. But the issue has not been avoided.

In August 1980, a mail survey of bar jurisdictions from the ABA's Division of Bar Services asked about the existence of alcohol abuse programs. Some 27 percent of those that replied claimed to have such programs; 46 percent of the responding state bar and 21 percent of the local bars did so. California's is the oldest of these programs, with Minnesota, Washington, and a handful of others following in the late 1970s (25).

Most bar association programs are nonprofit corporations, endorsed and supported by the organized bar, but functioning independently in order to preserve and maintain autonomy. Most feel that program success rests on airtight confidentiality. This is in marked contrast to the impaired physician committees which are usually very much a part of the state medical societies and which may either by law or by choice report a recalcitrant colleague to a licensing board (26).

In 1983, the Board of Governors of the Florida Bar approved in concept a new "impaired attorney rule" recommended by the Legal Standards Commission. If it achieves passage by the Florida Supreme Court, it will be the first of its kind in the United States. (It is printed in its entirety in the January 1983 issue of the *Florida Bar Journal*, an issue devoted almost wholly to articles on the impaired attorney issue.) The proposed legislation addresses the thorny problems inherent in intervention when an attorney is discovered to be impaired yet has not crossed the line so that an actual grievance against him exists. It attempts to balance due process with common sense and considers both the need to protect the public and the rights of the attorney involved (27).

Earlier, in 1980, Michael J. Hoover of the Lawyer's Professional Responsibility Board in St. Paul, Minnesota, had mailed a survey instrument to all American disciplinary councils. Twenty-four jurisdictions replied. They were asked about the number of disciplinary procedures in which an attorney's drinking was known or strongly suspected to be a major part of the problem. The relationship between alcoholism and disciplinary violations is high according to Hoover, with alcoholism involved in 10 percent or more of all grievances handled by disciplinary agencies. Its involvement is even higher in those cases where private discipline is imposed, rising to 15 or 20 percent in cases where public discipline and disbarment are imposed (28).

In 1977, Judge Leon Emerson of Downey, California, testified before the U.S. Senate Subcommittee on Alcoholism and Drug Abuse that "apparently 10–15% of our attorneys and judges are afflicted with the disease of alcoholism" (29). Begun in 1973, his pioneering California committee was then already active with about 300 cases, half of them self-referred and the other half threatened with disciplinary procedures and sent from the state bar association. The number of problem drinkers referred from disciplinary boards varies widely among states, with only 10 referred in 1979 in Minnesota, for instance; these numbers often reflect the referrals stemming from drunk driving convictions (30). The California Committee has developed their own 20-question self-test for alcoholic attorneys. (See Appendix D.)

In addition to the Florida effort, the ABA's Committee on Alcoholism and Drug Law Reform has been charged with the development of a model disciplinary rule to protect the confidentiality of existing programs and to set a policy on how best to handle the case of the alcoholic attorney. A survey being used in developing this rule has already raised some challenging questions:

1. Should a disciplinary procedure be stayed and the attorney diverted if substance abuse is an issue? Just for investigation? For treatment?

2. Should substance abuse be irrelevant in a disciplinary procedure until a sentence is chosen?

3. Are there offenses for which issues of addiction are totally irrelevant? (That is, if an alcoholic attorney kills a client, would the supreme court want to do more than just disbar?)

4. If alcoholism is raised as an issue by a disciplinary body or attorney, will there be a burden of proof and on whom should it rest? Need there be proof of accusation? (That is, is there a need to show that alcohol caused a dereliction of duty, or only the need to show an association of substance abuse and dereliction?) Should alcoholism alone be regarded as reason enough for a bar association to force treatment, or must one wait for an actual dereliction of duty?

These are not the only questions raised and many of these as well as others being studied are common to other professions. The ABA's rule will almost certainly prove useful to many others, particularly since the legal implications of setting up intervention programs and the moral dilemmas they inevitably raise have proved troublesome. As attorneys settle these matters for themselves, they are certain to be watched with intense interest. (See Advocacy versus Coercive Methods in Chapter 10.)

Meanwhile, a proliferation of local efforts and committees continues. Neither the Canadian Bar Association (CBA) nor its counterpart in Great Britain has announced official policy but, as in the United States, there has nevertheless been local activity. Particularly active is the Ontario Bar Alcoholism Program (OBAP). Endorsed by the Law Society of Upper Canada and the CBA-Ontario, but separate from them both, it offers special confidential assistance to Ontario lawyers and judges whose professional and personal lives are threatened by the impact of problems caused by alcoholism. In the absence of any national clearinghouse for information or any central listing of the many groups that exist and already attempt to assist attorneys, ILAA, OBAP, and LCL can all be consulted for help in locating others who can help. In the author's (LCB) experience, these attorneys have proven remarkably sensitive to issues of confidentiality as well as extremely resourceful and energetic when challenged with the opportunity to help a colleague in trouble. As mentioned in Chapter 7, the English Alcoholic Group for Lawyers (EAGL) is much like an English version of the ILAA.

SOCIAL WORK

In November of 1979, the Delegate Assembly of the National Association of Social Workers (NASW) approved a sophisticated and far-reaching policy statement on alcoholism and alcohol-related problems within the profession. It states that the social work profession can and should

> assume responsibility for examining the extent of alcohol problems within its own ranks and for taking appropriate measures to protect both the ill social workers and the patients whom they serve. Social workers suffering from alcoholism should be assured that treatment information and appropriate health benefits and safeguards are provided by institutions and agencies employing them, as well as by the profession of social work acting in its own behalf.

There was no further action on a national level until the fall of 1982 when a task force was appointed and charged with developing an EAP within NASW's national office and also with developing a plan and guidelines for impaired social workers. The National Occupational Social Work Task Force, as it was called, drew its members from those primarily interested in EAPs as a new career direction for social workers rather than from those employed more specifically in alcoholism, a situation which has left some concerned individuals uneasy (31).

There are plans to field test these guidelines for impaired social workers in Texas and Connecticut under a NASW Program Advancement Fund grant. Presently, no formal mechanism exists within the association for referring impaired professionals, but NASW Senior Staff Associate, Thomas Gautier, says the organization is prepared to assist, in a confidential manner, any individuals who wish to contact him at the national office.

In December of 1976, Christine Fewell, Barbara King, and other members of New York's NASW Committee on Alcoholism placed a questionnaire in *Currents,* the New York chapter's newsletter, asking about drinking among members (32). A total of 29 people responded, 20 of whom said they knew of one or more colleagues with drinking problems. Eleven had attempted a confrontation. The others had not and gave reasons (some giving more than one reason) for hesitating. The reasons included: 5 who were afraid the working relationship would be impaired, 4 who were afraid the person would be angry or that the person would see the concern as interfering, 2 who lacked knowledge about what to do, and the race issue was mentioned by 1. In addition, 4 said that the supervisor was the problem. Most said that they felt unsure of what to say or recommend. Some had tried to get a supervisor to help only to encounter denial on the part of the supervisor or to find that the supervisor was equally unsure of what to do (33).

Both the New York and New Jersey NASW chapters, who had jointly prepared the national policy statement, have already independently taken action—New Jersey with a hotline and New York with a Peer Consultation Committee established in May of 1979. The latter is a strictly confidential advocacy group and is linked to members of Social Workers Helping Social Workers. (See Appendix C.) Maryland and Massachusetts are also planning programs.

The New York City chapter of NASW in 1978 published a booklet entitled *Alcoholism among Social Workers, Approaching a Colleague with a Drinking Problem* (34). Well described by its title, this booklet is available from the New York chapter.

Thus far there have been very few self-referrals. New York and New Jersey have available many helping professionals, and social workers tend to know who they are, but they tend to turn to other professionals for help instead. There is the inevitable wariness about disclosure to a peer but, once issued, the license to practice social work is rarely threatened or revoked. Compared to about 900,000 physicians and twice that number of nurses, social workers are few in number and frequently serve out of role in a variety of settings. They are often not closely identified with other social workers or active in their professional organizations.

Formed in 1980 for mutual support and to help others, Social Workers Helping Social Workers (SWHSW) is open to all social workers with masters' degrees and to M.S.W. candidates with personal experience of alcoholism in their own lives or those of their families. (See Appendix C.) Its most rapid growth has been in the Midwest and on the eastern seaboard. John Fitzgerald, a former SWHSW chairperson, surveyed its membership and learned that 77 percent of their alcoholic members had never been approached about their problem in the workplace, although 87 percent indicated active abuse of a chemical during the workday; almost all reported "negative behaviors" at work that passed without comment. Included were being unable to read interview notes, using profane, insulting, or aggressive language, and making sexual overtures to a client (31).

An attempt to review the literature on all aspects of impairment in social workers revealed very little. Except for a 1980 study conducted by one of us (35), the studies mentioned above, and a brief description of social workers included in a hospital EAP, nothing could be located on the subject of alcoholism in this group.

PATTERNS OF RESPONSE

In most professions there has been a remarkably similar pattern of events. Initially, there is little attention paid to the individual in trouble, even though colleagues may know of a problem. It is assumed that such cases are rare. Next, a significant number achieve recovery without the help of their peers, usually through A.A. or through A.A. plus other helping individuals or agencies.

Since A.A. charges its members with "carrying the message to other alcoholics," these people quite logically wish to become advocates for their peers. Individual efforts to influence hierarchies usually fail, so groups of "recovereds" develop within the different professions in order to provide social contacts, networking, support, and, usually later, a formal organization that adopts outreach programs and ways of disseminating information to other colleagues. The group and the professional organization then work more or less in harmony to devise formal policy statements and programs. While both recovered alcoholics and their nonalcoholic colleagues are limited in what each group can do in isolation, they can complement each other's strengths effectively if they are willing to do so. At first there is frequently mistrust and battling over who will control and who will take credit and who will be spokesperson, particularly since these efforts may be of considerable interest to the media and may offer the members of "impairment" committees a tempting opportunity to compete for the limelight. Usually, the less public the identity of individual committee members, the better.

One of us (LCB) was fortunate enough to observe the early formation of several of these groups, those composed of social workers and psychologists, to be in on some of the discussions that subsequently led to the formation of ILAA and to watch an attempt to establish a group for nurses similar to that for social workers. (Unfortunately, this last mentioned effort failed, at least that time.) While each profession has its own distinct style and way of addressing or avoiding a problem, the similarities are striking. Other organizations will predictably follow similar paths, but they will increasingly have available to them the information and experiences of professional organizations that have learned by trial and error.

REFERENCES

1. R. G. Niven, "Physicians Perceptions and Attitudes towards Disabled Colleagues," in: *The Impaired Physician, Proceedings of the Third Annual Conference on the Impaired Physician*, Minneapolis, Minn., 1978, Chicago: Department of Mental Health, American Medical Association, 1980, pp. 21–26.

2. R. J. Smith and E. M. Steindler, "The Psychiatric Gap in Impaired Physician Programs," *Psychiatric Annals 12*: 1982, pp. 207–24.

3. American Medical Association, Council on Mental Health, "The Sick Physician," *Journal of the American Medical Association 223*: February 5, 1973, pp. 684–87.

4. Available from Health & Human Behavior Program, American Medical Association, 535 N. Dearborn St., Chicago, Ill. 60610.

5. *1982–83 Yearbook and Directory of Osteopathic Physicians*, Chicago: American Osteopathic Association, 1982, p. 399.

6. R. E. Jones, "Specialty Society Involvement—American Psychiatric Association," in: *The Impaired Physician: Building Well-Being, Proceedings of the Fourth Annual Conference on the Impaired Physician*, Baltimore, 1980, Chicago: Department of Mental Health, American Medical Association, 1981, pp. 17–19.

7. D. M. Keith, "Specialty Society Involvement—American Academy of Family Physicians," ibid., pp. 19–20.

8. L. J. Shulman, "Specialty Society Involvement—American College of Obstetricians and Gynecologists," ibid., pp. 21–22.

9. F. Asma, Personal Communication, 1983.

10. National Council on Alcoholism, "Criteria for the Diagnosis of Alcoholism," *Annals of Internal Medicine 77*: 1972, pp. 249–58.

11. "Rehabilitating the Impaired Dentist," *Journal of the American Dental Association 105*: 1982, pp. 781–87.

12. H. R. Hedge, "Recovering Alcoholic Dentists, A Preliminary Survey," *Iowa Dental Journal 68*: July 1982, pp. 41–42.

13. R. E. Herrington et al., "Treating Substance Use Disorders among Physicians," *Journal of the American Medical Association 247*: April 23–30, 1982, pp. 2253–57.

14. F. Wamsley, "Dentistry Through a Glass Darkly," *Dental Management 18*: November 1978, pp. 27–34.

15. D. K. Cassell, "Understanding the Alcoholic Dentist," *Dental Economics 68*: February 1978, pp. 52–57.

16. "A Commitment Towards Helping Others" (editorial), *Connecticut State Dental Association Journal 54*: 1980, p. 138.

17. "The Connecticut State Dental Association and the Committee on Drug and Alcohol Abuse," ibid., pp. 143–44.

18. "Alcohol—Drugs—Nitrous Oxide, Worried?" ibid., p. 148.

19. J. Klemesrud, "The Alcoholic Nurse: Facing the Problem," *New York Times*, March 11, 1978.

20. C. Isler, "The Alcoholic Nurse. What We Try to Deny," *RN 41*: 1978, pp. 48–55.

21. American Nurses' Association, Resolutions Committee, Resolution 5, "Action on Alcohol and Drug Misuse and Psychological Dysfunctions among Nurses," 1982.

22. "Help for the Helper," *American Journal of Nursing 82*: April 1982, pp. 572–87.

23. C. F. Ward et al., "Drug Abuse in Anesthesia Training Programs, A Survey: 1970 Through 1980," *Journal of the American Medical Association 250*: August 19, 1983, pp. 922–25.

24. V. Castleberry, "Nurses Get Little Help with Drug-Related Problems," *Dallas Times Herald*, September 25, 1983, pp. 1, 3.

25. M. Middleton, "Help, Hope for the Alcoholic Lawyer," *Bar Leader 6*: January–February 1981, pp. 29–30.

26. B. Alexander, "The Disease of Addiction from the Pillory to Medicare," *Florida Bar Journal 57*: 1983, pp. 21–26.

27. C. R. Muller, "A New Approach to an Old Problem," ibid., pp. 33–38.

28. M. J. Hoover, "Final Results of Survey of Disciplinary Council Concerning Alcoholism," St. Paul, Minn.: Lawyers' Professional Responsibility Board, 1980, pp. 33–57.

29. U.S. Senate Committee on Human Resources, Subcommittee on Alcoholism and Drug Abuse, *Congressional Record*, 1977.

30. W. Winter, "Alcoholic Lawyers: The Probation Option," *Bar Leader 5*: January–February 1980, p. 27.

31. "Impaired Workers Program in the Works," *National Association of Social Workers News 28*: September 1983, p. 17.

32. "Alcoholism—Problem among Colleagues?" *Currents* (New York Chapter, National Association of Social Workers Newsletter), December 1976, p. 5.

33. C. Fewell and B. L. King, Personal Communication, 1977.

34. *Alcoholism among Social Workers, Approaching a Colleague with a Drinking Problem*, New York: National Association of Social Workers, New York City Chapter, 1978.

35. L. Bissell et al., "The Alcoholic Social Worker, A Survey," *Social Work in Health Care 5*: Summer 1980, pp. 421–32.

9

The Response of Other Professions

In the previous chapter, we describe what the professional organizations that represent the five occupational groups we interviewed have done to address alcoholism in their membership. In Chapter 10, we discuss some other approaches developed within these same and other disciplines, as well as some general considerations that should be common to the planning phase of any program for impaired members in any of the professions.

There are many other important professions we might equally well have studied. For some of them there is available information about alcoholism in their ranks. What follows is a brief description of some of the things we found and a survey of the existing literature, albeit elusive and still quite limited. We will also try to indicate those factors peculiar to a given occupation that have been mentioned to us as perhaps needing of special understanding.

Employee assistance programs (EAPs) and self-help groups for alcoholic women were developed later than those for men. In a 1979 survey of nearly 800 counselors, most of them employed by EAPs, and others frequently referring patients to residential treatment (1) the respondents said that only 10 percent of alcoholics they had referred were women—a number disproportionate to the female presence in the workplace. In 1982, a survey of 365 EAPs showed that only 18 percent of those served by drug or alcohol programs were women, although 35 percent of those employed by the sponsor companies were females (2).

Within occupations, those that have proportionately more women have developed alcoholism programs more slowly than those whose members are largely male. This has been the case both within industry and within the professions and irrespective of whether union or management predominates in establishing them. Thus we see programs for flight attendants founded eight years after those for airline pilots, nurses lagging well behind physicians, garment workers trailing seamen and longshoremen, teachers and librarians relatively unserved when compared to doctors and attorneys.

Part of the reason for this may be that alcoholism is still often perceived as largely a male condition. Even today, the incidence among women is probably seriously underestimated, even by women themselves. An additional problem for a number of professions is certainly money. Nurses, librarians, and teachers, most of them women, most of them notoriously underpaid when compared to men with equivalent years of education, lack the available funds to travel, to meet, and to organize. Weekend conventions on alcohol-related problems for doctors and attorneys in the United States can even be attended by physicians and lawyers from Great Britain with relative ease. A similar meeting for nurses or social workers represents a much greater personal investment and may not be feasible.

CLERGY

Responses to the needs of alcoholic clergy have varied widely among the religious denominations, and even within the same denomination, as well as in different parts of the country.

Episcopal

Within the Episcopal Church, the Recovered Alcoholic Clergy Association (RACA) came into being after repeated attempts to persuade its General Convention to establish a churchwide alcoholism program had failed and its Advisory Committee on Alcoholism had disbanded in 1967. The following year, Rev. James T. Golder of San Francisco appealed to other recovered alcoholic clergy to contact him. In October of 1968, 6 of the 22 respondents had met and organized RACA—a name chosen for its biblical connotations (see Matthew, 5:22). By 1979, there were about 200 members and, in 1979, the General Convention of the Episcopal Church resolved to request each diocese to develop a written procedure for treatment of clergy and members of their families who suffer from the illness of alcoholism (3).

The resolution notes that "alcoholism is a serious and fatal disease if left untreated; it is also a treatable illness with excellent prognosis for recovery." Each diocese was asked to include in its policy a statement covering the use of alcoholic beverages at church functions and on church property. One of the results of this policy, a small brochure entitled *Guidelines for the Use of Alcoholic Beverages at Church Functions and on Church Property Within the Diocese of Maryland* (March 1981), by the Rt. Rev. David K. Leighton, D.D., offers one of the most thoughtful and practical approaches anywhere in print, accepting of the fact that people are going to drink, while suggesting concrete ways to avoid most of the negative consequences (4).

In *Alcoholism and the Church, a Call to Action*, a pamphlet distributed to Anglican clergy describing the resolution made by the General Convention and suggesting ways in which to make it effective (3), Rev. Vernon Johnson states that

> all the other helping professions operate under the ethic that the sick must come to them and ask for aid. Contrariwise, by the Divine Command implicit in ordination, the clergy is sent to search out the sick and needy and to minister to them . . . to comb the hedges and the highways and . . . compel them to come in.

He goes on to explain that alcoholics, by the very nature of their disease, are incapable of recognizing its severity spontaneously, so that "intervention is the norm rather than the exception." Defined as "presenting reality to a person out of touch with it in a reasonable way," guidelines on intervention techniques are offered, which are essentially the same, whether the person in need is colleague or parishioner.

Roman Catholic

Although the Catholic National Clergy Council on Alcoholism (NCCA) is now 35 years old, as recently as 1976 only about 20 percent of the dioceses had implemented its practices and recommendations. It has for many years recommended a pragmatic approach to the problem of alcoholism among church personnel and distributed copies of a recommended program to every diocese in the United States. Among several reasons for the sluggish response, Fichter suggests, are difficulty in recognizing the problem, a feeling that "excessive drinking is immoral and scandalous and should be kept quiet," being too busy with other diocesan matters perceived as more urgent, and reluctance to examine one's own pattern of alcohol consumption (5).

Both Anglican and Catholic bishops enjoy considerable autonomy and are relatively free to handle problem priests as they think best. Some know very little about it; others, a great deal. Some have themselves recovered from alcoholism. The Catholic bishop is expected to regard his priests as "sons and friends" and should always have a "special love" as well as a "trusting familiarity" for them. If the diocese is seen as a familial rather than as a work organization, the fatherly authority of the bishop cannot be exercised in the same businesslike manner as is the authority of the company executive (5,6). Religious orders and even different communities within an order are able to set their own policies, and the Catholic Church as a whole has never made an official policy statement about alcoholism in its ranks. Because of its polity, it is unlikely to do so.

According to Dr. George Gallup in a 1979 address to United Presbyterian Church leaders (7), the proportion of drinkers among clergy is lower than that for the general population, with only 50 percent of the clergy polled by his organization reporting any use of alcoholic beverages as opposed to 70 percent for the population as a whole. One-third said they received no seminary training to help them deal with alcoholism or other alcohol-related problems. The proportion who said that liquor at one point or another was a cause of trouble in their immediate families was not far below the proportion for the rest of the public.

Alcoholism has frequently been noted to be less common

among Jews and those of the Mediterranean cultures than among other ethnic groups (8). There is a cherished belief that Jews therefore escape it altogether. "Shikker vie ein goy" (the drunkard is a gentile) is part of the folklore. Dr. Sheila Blume even told us of a rabbi who, when faced with one of his congregation who insisted that he was alcoholic, replied with some disdain, "Are you sure you know who your father is?" Rabbis have been slow to appear in A.A. and in treatment centers but they are there in growing numbers and the JACS (Jewish Alcoholics, Chemical Dependents and Significant Others) Foundation, which attempts to reach alcoholic Jews through the rabbinate, will inevitably help to educate the helpers as well.

Other denominations vary widely as to what they have done. The Lutheran Church has been active and doubtless others have as well, but clergy have been understandably hesitant to invite publicity. (As one put it, "The gynecologist isn't supposed to get VD himself, so you try to handle it somehow but keep it quiet.") The ecumenical movement has concentrated its attention on joint efforts to help parishioners with alcoholism rather than the clergy themselves.

Division among church leaders even within a given denomination on the issue of abstinence can contribute to a stalemate. Some denominations suggest or require abstinence as a condition of membership, while others sanction moderate alcohol use. The Mormon or Southern Baptist who admits to a drinking problem is in double jeopardy, since all drinking is prohibited in the first place. Bad enough for a layperson, much worse for the clergy! Even those denominations who espouse "responsible use" often are said to "act wet and talk dry." Rarely does one hear a television evangelist make a statement one way or the other about drinking in general, no matter how often the more extreme behaviors such as drunk driving or drinking by children are lamented. Regardless of the reason, many churches have found it just as well not to insist too loudly on the presence of alcoholic clergy in their ranks nor to organize on their behalf.

The Hazelden Rehabilitation Center reported on 214 religious professionals admitted for treatment between 1973 and 1976 (9). These subjects did not differ substantially from the other non-medical professionals described in their sample with regard to age at admission or use of other drugs. None had used narcotics. They proved less likely to be married (many were Catholic, and some were nuns and brothers) and, after discharge, only slightly less likely to be members of A.A. The reported treatment outcome of no further drinking whatsoever for 12 months after discharge was also comparable to the other professionals as well as to the treatment outcome Fichter reports for clergy treated in facilities serving only clergy—30 percent of Fichter's group and 31 percent of the Hazelden religious professionals (10).

EDUCATION

Organizations of teachers and of college faculty are not exactly analogous to those serving the occupational groups previously described. They see their role as more like that of a union and their task primarily as one designed to protect members against arbitrary and unfair attack more than as one in which they set standards for and attempt to regulate members' behavior.

The American Association of University Professors has no formal policy statement dealing with alcoholic faculty. However, according to Associate General Secretary Jordan Kirkland, they have worked with institutions to assure due process before dismissal for alcoholism. They consider it a medical problem and seek remedial action before termination results from incompetence, neglect, or misconduct.

In 1976, the National Institute for Alcohol Abuse and Alcoholism awarded what was to be a seven-year grant to the University of Missouri at Columbia for an employee assistance program primarily targeted to faculty. This demonstration project has been continued on a smaller scale by the university, still has available material to share with other colleges and universities, and has in press a book describing the project (11,12).

At the university, noncoercive self-help groups, designed along the lines of the Lawyers Concerned for Lawyers group or the Dentists Concerned for Dentists group, exist for what are primarily graduate school faculty, and there are some on-campus A.A. meetings attended largely by faculty as well. Among the former are Anthropologists Concerned for Anthropologists (extant since 1981) and Sociologists Concerned for Sociologists. (See Appendix C.)

A recent film designed for department chairpersons, deans, superintendents, principals, and administrators uses a male college professor as the alcoholic protagonist (13). There have been alcoholism programs established rather sporadically in college and school systems, sometimes quite explicitly dealing with alcoholism, as in the case of Montgomery County, Maryland, and other times more informally, as at Brown University where former classics department head, Bruce Donovan, carries the title of Associate Dean with Special Responsibilities in the Area of Chemical Dependence (14). These campus efforts are still few in number—45 active EAPs in higher education in 27 states as of 1981 (15) and the literature sparse. In the foreword to *The Last Bell Is Ringing*, one of the very few writings available on alcoholism among teachers (16), author-educator Robert Russell sees "the education profession . . . unlikely at this time [1976] to be open to any such program"; later in a March 1979 article he reports that little still had been done (17).

In any discussion of alcoholism in academia, two considerations arise at once, tenure and academic freedom. If one appears to challenge either of these, the faculty presents a united front of resistance. A standard EAP approach based on job performance and hierarchy is predestined to failure. Faculty do not see themselves as employees in the first place. Hours and place of work are extremely flexible, so that many are on campus only a few hours per week and much office work is done at home.

Approaches through administration swiftly reveal that, while the authority structure may on paper resemble that of a corporation, in its actual functioning it is not. Few administrators would challenge a united stand by an academic senate. A chairperson or department head may also prove helpless to start a new program that colleagues may label as authoritarian or infringing on their freedom. Often the department head's position rotates at regular intervals and decisions get made based on the consensus of the tenured professors who are department members.

Faculty members often see themselves as the last holdouts on the value of the individual and individual judgment. Supportive of the creative maverick and nonconformist, they resist interference from above as a matter of principle. Furthermore, drinking has long been fashionable on most college campuses. William Madsen once described college drinking customs for an alcoholic trying to abstain as being as "precarious as walking a greased tightrope while blindfolded over a den of rattlesnakes. Tolerance is increasing but the abstainer is . . . an outsider to many of the more intensive professional recreational activities" (18).

LIBRARY SCIENCE

As of late 1983, The American Library Association had neither issued a policy statement on alcoholism nor instituted a program for its members. Deputy Director Ruth Frane said that, in response to members' requests, the phone number of an A.A. contact plus some general information have been included in conference program announcements (19). There has also been a review of group health insurance coverage with an eye to ensuring access to alcoholism treatment should it be needed. She went on to volunteer that since librarians are 80 percent women and alcoholism is more common in males, there is probably less of a problem than in other fields. If rates are adjusted for sex, she does not believe that they will differ from those found in the general population.

Individual library systems might well have instituted EAPs that include librarians along with all other staff. This is the case at the Library of Congress, although data about how many professional librarians do use this and similar services are not currently available. Universities may have done the same. Calls to members of a group of librarians who are information specialists in alcoholism and substance abuse found them unable to name any such programs, and several volunteered that they would certainly have remembered seeing any such information.

The New York Public Library has recently explored the feasibility of a program for their staff but has not yet decided exactly when or if they will start one. Meanwhile, most of their staff are included in a union-based program, Local 37-B, which provides alcoholism counseling to workers in a variety of work settings. There is no way to know, because of confidentiality considerations, whether or not any professional librarians have tried to use this service; it is not unusual for EAPs to be available to and used by support staff, while this is not true for professionals working in the same setting.

PHARMACY

In April 1982, the American Pharmaceutical Association's House of Delegates adopted as policy "that pharmacists should not practice while subject to . . . impairment due to . . . drugs—

including alcohol" and supported "establishment of counseling, treatment, prevention and rehabilitation programs for pharmacists and pharmacy students who are subject to physical or mental impairment due to the influence of drugs—including alcohol . . ." (20).

Several state pharmaceutical associations have already established rehabilitation committees. Indiana has been active since 1979, for example, and Texas maintains a confidential "Helpline" with an "800" number. Committees in Maryland and Minnesota are already operational, and journal articles on impaired pharmacists have also begun to appear (21,22). "Dr. Paul," writing in the April 1982 *American Pharmacy*, discusses a hotline for impaired pharmacists.

On June 7, 1983, Dr. Richard Penna, of the American Pharmaceutical Association, launched what is planned to be an annual course at the University of Utah's School of Alcohol Studies. The school for several years has included a section for pharmacists that concentrates on alcohol and drug problems in general, but Penna has combined some of the original content with state of the art information specifically addressed to the needs and problems of the drug- and alcohol-dependent pharmacist, drawing together those pharmacists most concerned with helping their colleagues. Penna hopes to continue this for several years until guidelines are well developed, procedures polished, and the profession more aware of both problems and solutions. Placing this activity in the midst of an ongoing school permits the borrowing of experts from other sections who then become faculty for the pharmacists at little additional cost.

A new problem reported by members of this student body is the growing, though still apparently small, number of pharmacy students who not only are involved with drugs prior to entering professional school, but who are choosing a career in pharmacy in hopes of having access to them. Because pharmacists work and train in a milieu where inevitably they must concern themselves with narcotics and other tightly regulated drugs, they are very aware of the record keeping, prescribing, and distribution patterns needed for these agents. They are very alert to the temptations posed to themselves and their colleagues by controlled drugs. Unfortunately, the noise and attention surrounding narcotics and cocaine have drowned out much of what might otherwise have been heard about alcoholism, and the profession has only recently become more aware of alcohol-related problems.

PSYCHOLOGY

In March 1981, a group of 14 concerned psychologists from Illinois, Michigan, New York, Missouri, Connecticut, and Rhode Island met for three days in New England to consider the problems of the alcoholic and chemically dependent psychologist. At this time, Psychologists Helping Psychologists (PHP)—an advocacy, networking, and support group open to recovered alcoholic, doctoral-level psychologists—was organized. Soon thereafter this group got in touch with Richard Kilberg of the American Psychological Association (APA), offering to assist in outreach programs for colleagues still in need of help.

In October 1980, APA's Board of Professional Affairs was asked by the APA Council on Representatives to consider a resolution on "distressed psychologists." It voted instead to study existing data and to allocate an hour of convention time to the subject (23). This was done in 1981, and then again in 1982 and 1983, with PHP also on the agenda.

The APA does not yet have a formal statement or policy regarding alcoholism among its 57,000 members. Allegedly this is because members felt that to have one for alcoholism would oblige them to have separate policies for other specific impairments, such as depression, and that would be an overwhelming task. However, a steering committee of three men was appointed in August 1981. It is charged with developing a proposal for helping psychologists with a variety of impairments for eventual presentation to the board. Still under discussion is the establishment of "VIP" (Volunteers in Psychology), a nonprofit organization that might be designed to offer information and referral services and to utilize a networking format with an "800" number which is to be manned by volunteers.

A search of the literature revealed only two articles in print specifically on the subject of the alcoholic psychologist, both authored by Dr. Jane Skorina (24,25), who is also the contact person for PHP; although PHP developed and remained outside of the professional organization, it is now in liaison with the steering committee mentioned above. (See Appendix C.) Dr. Skorina does not claim that psychologists are at particularly high risk of developing alcoholism, but she does state that her discipline's approach to the problem may well make it more difficult for an individual to acknowledge its presence or to admit the need to abstain.

Certainly the way in which alcoholism is conceptualized will influence what one attempts to do about it. If it is seen as a learned behavior or set of habits, however dysfunctional, then it is reasonable to attempt to unlearn it and replace it with something else. If it is seen as an irreversible illness that, once firmly established, can be managed only through abstinence, the task is very different (26). While most physicians seem comfortable with this latter approach, many psychologists still feel that controlled drinking is a reasonable goal. It is primarily among their ranks that this view is still held and among themselves that some of the most heated battles on this issue occur (27). Committed to behavioral change and to a belief in their own power to solve problems and to effect change in themselves and others, psychologists may heroically resist acknowledging a limitation in themselves.

In addition to the barriers common to all mental health professionals when it comes to seeking and accepting help, Skorina notes others that probably make psychologists particularly hard to reach (28). The most typical places of employment for psychologists are academia and private practice, so that all of the protections of the tenure system designed to permit freedom and diversity of expression are equally suitable for fending off intervention in the case of a deteriorating job performance. Usually there is little close supervision, and those most likely to be aware of questionable behavior are those with the least power to do anything about it—students and patients. Psychologists have themselves frequently used both drugs and alcohol (in many cases encouraged by other members of the profession) in an attempt to expand consciousness and to ferret out more knowledge of all matters of the mind (29). Collegial protection among these professionals is almost impenetrable and carries with it the strong agreement not to interfere with or impinge on the freedom of a colleague.

While every group has its own cultural myth about alcoholism, psychology is particularly adept at obfuscating, questioning, examining, and challenging any delineating factors that would permit clarity in diagnosis and a sure-handed direction into treatment. The reach for scientific purity, the attempt to avoid rigidity, and oversimplification can result in paralysis. Skorina notes a compulsion to define absolutes even when absolutes are undefinable (28). As she puts it, psychologists, trained to analyze their research, their patients, and themselves objectively, use that training to facilitate their own denial "as data are collected and collected and collected. . . . Only to be analyzed and analyzed and analyzed . . . an attempt . . . to come to omnipotent conclusions, but only to obsess."

Perhaps even more than other disciplines, psychology will benefit from the rapidly increasing body of knowledge concerning brain function and alcoholism. If convinced that courage and insight cannot reasonably be expected to triumph over physiology (particularly when judgment and self-awareness are seriously compromised by the action of the drug itself), they may more easily permit themselves to acknowledge defeat. If psychologists can be freed of the notion that this impairment (alcoholism) is a narcissistic injury and see it instead as more analogous to an allergy, they may become truly free from alcohol. One can then opt out of the struggle for control which, even when successful, tends to leave alcoholics still entrapped by alcohol, although in a different way, with much of their energy still engaged by the battle. Dr. Ernest Kurtz' book, *Not God* (30,31), is a favorite with psychologists interested in alcoholism, especially because it makes clear and interprets the therapeutic dynamics underlying the success of A.A. in understandable terms of established psychological principles and procedures.

VETERINARY MEDICINE

A letter to the Executive Vice-President of the American Veterinary Medical Association in 1980 asking about alcoholism in this profession brought a candid reply of "we just don't know" (32). He knew of licenses being revoked or suspended because of drug abuse, but did not know about much of a problem. As of 1983, there was no formal policy statement, procedure, or program, but the House of Delegates recently adopted a resolution calling for the Association ". . . to establish a committee to investigate current State and national diversion programs for impaired physicians and other professionals for the purpose of developing similar programs for veterinarians, either separately or in conjunction with existing ones" (33).

A number of veterinarians attend and are welcome members of IDAA, where individuals suggest that not only is alcoholism present, as it is in all professions, but that there is one factor that is unique in this discipline. The person practicing veterinary medicine not only has the same access to drugs as the physician or dentist but in addition may be working with large animals who require proportionately large quantities of drugs and who are not going to be able to report how much discomfort they felt or whether the medication was actually given. This gives the veterinarian an excellent opportunity to divert drugs without much chance of detection.

In common with many other professionals who tend to be in solo rather than group practice, most veterinarians work with little or no supervision and, even though they do highly sophisticated surgery, their assistants are not nurses who report to an independent nursing office but are more likely to be hired and trained by the doctor doing the surgery. These co-workers are not usually in regular contact with others doing similar work and are ignorant as to how to report their concerns and realistically afraid of being fired if they do. It is no surprise that relatively few addiction problems actually surface. The need to work irregular hours in order to handle emergencies provides a ready excuse for any missed appointments, and there may be few if any times when colleagues are consulted about schedules.

One Texas veterinarian who has recovered from alcoholism and addiction to a wide assortment of other drugs is also convinced that his colleagues may be at highest risk of drug addiction when compared to all other medical professions—as well as the least likely to be detected. They may well be the group about which it will prove most difficult to learn whether or not he is correct.

THE RESPONSE OF THE BUSINESS COMMUNITY AND INDUSTRY

Many corporations have "industrial" alcoholism programs or EAPs. Dupont, Eastman Kodak, *The New York Times*, Allis Chalmers, and Illinois Bell, for example, have had programs for many years that identify alcoholism in the workplace and that refer employees for treatment when job performance deteriorates. As long as work remains unaffected, management regards the employees' decisions about drinking as a private matter. When work is affected, drinking becomes the employer's concern and action can be taken, with the threat of job loss used, if necessary, to coerce treatment—just as a doctor's or nurse's license can be revoked or a lawyer disbarred.

Members of professional groups and those in sensitive occupations have been slower to take action than the business community. For these groups, the very considerations that make it important that problems be faced squarely and promptly make it more difficult to admit that the problem of alcoholism exists. However, the U.S. State Department now has an excellent program. So do the C.I.A. and the Air Line Pilots Association (ALPA), as do occupations as varied as longshoremen, police, flight attendants, and merchant seamen.

In comparison, the health-care industry, if regarded as a whole, is probably the nation's second largest industry, and yet it lags far behind (34). Few hospitals see themselves as industries; few have programs for their own employees; and relatively few groups of health professionals have developed effective systems for reaching out to their colleagues.

REFERENCES

1. L. Bissell and S. Johnson, "Great Expectations—Families and Treatment," paper presented at National Council on Alcoholism, Annual Forum, Seattle, May 1980.

2. S. IntVeldt, "Effects on Program Utilization," *ALMACAN 13*: August 1983, pp. 3, 7.

3. *Alcoholism and the Church, A Call to Action*, New York: The Church Pension Fund (Episcopal Church), 1979.

4. D. K. Leighton, *Guidelines for the Use of Alcoholic Beverages at Church Functions on Church Property within the Diocese of Maryland*, March 1981.

5. J. H. Fichter, "Alcohol Addiction: Priests and Prelates," *America 137*: October 22, 1977, pp. 258–60.

6. J. H. Fichter, *The Rehabilitation of Clergy Alcoholics*, New York: Human Sciences Press, 1982.

7. *Monday Morning Report*, The American Business Men's Research Foundation, Lansing, Mich.: August 6, 1979.

8. C. R. Snyder, *Alcohol and the Jews*, New Haven, Conn.: Yale Center of Alcohol Studies, 1958.

9. J. Spicer and P. Barnett, "Characteristics and Outcomes of Professionals Admitted to the Hazelden Rehabilitation Center, 1973–1976," Center City, Minn.: Hazelden, 1978.

10. J. H. Fichter, "Ardent Spirits Subdued," in: *The Occupational Connection, Proceedings of the 15th Annual Eagleville Conference*, Eagleville, Pa.: May 1982, pp. 222–29.

11. Requests to Richard W. Thoresen, Ph.D., 320 Student Union Building, University of Missouri, Columbia, Missouri 65211.

12. E. A. Hosokowa and R. W. Thoresen, *Employee Assistance Programming in Higher Education*, New York: Charles C Thomas (in press).

13. "E.A.P. for Educators" (film), Hartsdale, N.Y.: Motivision Ltd., 1983.

14. Celebrity Spotlight, *Alcoholism Update 5*: April–June 1982, pp. 1, 3, 6.

15. Provost for Academic Affairs, Director of Personnel and Employee Relations, "E.A.P. Fact Sheet," University of Missouri, Columbia.

16. R. D. Russell, *The Last Bell Is Ringing*, Chicago: Midwestern Area Alcohol Education and Training Program, Inc., 1976.

17. R. D. Russell, "Problem Drinking in the Education Profession," *Phi Delta Kappan*: March 1979, pp. 506–9.

18. W. Madsen, presentation at the Conference on Alcoholism Programming in Academia, sponsored by University of Missouri, Newport, R.I., 1979.

19. R. Frane, Personal Communication, 1983.

20. "Editorial and Viewpoint," *American Pharmacy 22*: April 1982, pp. 5–7; "Professional Affairs," *American Pharmacy*: July 1982, p. 368.

21. S. Lerner, "The Alcohol-Impaired Pharmacist: The Profession Needs a Policy," *American Pharmacy 22*: April 1982, pp. 174–76.

22. R. Brody, "The Story Behind a Pharmacist Who Got Hooked on Rx Drugs," *American Druggist 179*: April 1979, pp. 32–36.

23. R. W. Thoresen et al., "The Alcoholic Psychologist: Issues, Problems and Implications for the Profession," *Professional Psychology: Research and Practice* (in press).

24. J. K. Skorina, "Alcoholic Psychologists: The Need for Humane and Effective Regulation," *Professional Practice of Psychology 3*: (2) 1982, pp. 33–41.

25. ———, "The Alcoholic Psychologist," *Focus on Alcohol and Drug Issues 5*: May–June 1982, pp. 11–14.

26. L. Bissell, *Some Perspectives on Alcoholism: A Professional's Guide*, Minneapolis, Minn.: Johnson Institute, 1982.

27. M. Pendery et al., "Controlled Drinking by Alcoholics? New Findings and a Reevaluation of a Major Affirmative Study," *Science 217*: 1982, pp. 169–75.

28. J. K. Skorina, "The Alcoholic Psychologist: Professional Considerations," paper presented at 91st annual convention of the American Psychological Association, Anaheim, Calif., 1983.

29. A. Weil, *The Natural Mind, a New Way of Looking at Drugs and the Higher Consciousness*, Boston: Houghton-Mifflin, 1972.

30. E. Kurtz, *Not God: A History of Alcoholics Anonymous*, Center City, Minn.: Hazelden, 1979.

31. E. Kurtz, "Why AA Works: The Intellectual Significance of Alcoholics Anonymous," *Journal of Studies on Alcohol 43*: 1982, pp. 38–80.

32. D. A. Price, American Veterinary Medical Association, Personal Communication, 1980.

33. American Veterinary Medical Association, 120th annual meeting, New York, Resolution 6, p. 100 (Business Section), July 1983.

34. G. Jackson, "An Employee Alcoholism Program for Nurses and Social Workers," *Labor-Management Alcoholism Journal 9*: November–December 1979, pp. 115–22.

10

Recommendations for Action

Long before an alcoholic professional comes to the attention of a state committee or licensing board, it should be apparent to family and co-workers that there is a problem. In the case of a hospital, its staff and even its trustees can be held liable in malpractice actions, hence there are business reasons as well as ethical and humanitarian ones for acting on the awareness of a colleague's drinking problem. Standards of the Joint Commission on Accreditation of Hospitals urge regular review of a physician's competence though not of the staff. In addition, according to the laws of some states (e.g., New York's "snitch law" for physicians and its counterpart for nurses in Florida), professionals can lose their own license to practice if they fail to report any colleagues they believe to be dangerous.

If we accept that early intervention in the process of any disease is desirable, then plans can be made that encourage early case finding and remedial action. If we also accept that alcoholism rarely appears overnight and that early deviations from the norm may be subtle and inconspicuous, then family and close friends are likely to be the first to suspect that something is awry. They need to know of available resources where they can sort out whether or not their concern is warranted and learn how to proceed if it is. Many EAPs within industry mail brochures to the homes of all employees describing and offering their services.

Confidentiality is stressed and honored. Medical society auxiliary members are sometimes sent similar materials. Quite often problems are voluntarily handled through these informal systems alone.

Committees can be formed within hospitals, agencies, companies, or other work settings and charged with first helping by informally suggesting treatment and later, if softer measures fail, by compelling the alcoholic to seek help. Early, well-planned intervention is obviously more sensible than delay while waiting for a disaster or for a miraculous solution to an obviously worsening problem. Alcoholism has been called a progressive disease because it usually becomes more serious with the passage of time. If early intervention can avoid legal and governmental confrontation altogether, so much the better. Planning for alcoholic physicians, nurses, and social workers or for judges, attorneys, and law clerks should logically be part of an overall plan for the total hospital staff or for that of an entire law firm; trustees, technicians, and administrators also get sick.

DEFINITION OF PROBLEMS

In approaching the alcoholic, regardless of the setting in which this is done, a clear understanding of problem professionals in general is necessary. For convenience, they can be divided into three categories.

1. *The incompetent.* This category includes those who were initially poorly trained or who have failed to keep their knowledge of their field current. The problem is one addressed through improved examination and evaluation procedures for both American and foreign graduates, development of periodic relicensing or recertifying procedures, and continuing education efforts designed to prevent obsolescence of skills. This is basically a gate-keeping and quality-control issue.

2. *The unethical.* Individuals who are simply dishonest or uncaring about the welfare of others. Included here can be the "script doctors" who knowingly prescribe addictive but technically legal drugs primarily for money. Also included are those who subject patients to unnecessary tests, procedures, or surgery or engage in a variety of other unsavory profit-making schemes, such as running "medicaid mills," entering into conflict-of-interest

arrangements, agreeing to bring frivolous law suits, practicing fee-splitting, and the like. These problems require appropriate disciplinary procedures.

3. *The impaired.* This group includes those who can best be regarded as ill rather than malicious or uninformed. They can be subdivided into two categories.

A.   Those who cannot reasonably be expected to recover from their illness (although no one should be regarded as hopeless without certainty that this is the case). This category would include, for example, those with irreversible organic brain syndrome or those with sensory impairments too severe to permit responsible functioning. These colleagues must be stopped, kindly but firmly, from practicing.

B.   Those who can reasonably be expected to recover if appropriately treated. Fortunately, this second category includes most of the alcoholic and otherwise addicted professionals as well as many of the mentally ill. It is not uncommon to find someone regarded as senile who is actually deeply depressed, drugged, or suffering from an entirely treatable metabolic derangement—in one series of presumably senile physicians, 21 of 32 were found to have been so misdiagnosed (1). While heavy social drinking short of actual alcoholism has been shown to cause brain damage even in the absence of malnutrition, most of it is entirely reversible with abstinence. The approach needed for this group is diagnosis, not accusation. One must arrange treatment rather than discipline or reeducation.

TREATMENT CONSIDERATIONS

There is no longer much debate about the goals of treatment for an alcoholic. The road must lead to abstinence from alcohol as well as all other mood-changing drugs of addiction. Membership in Alcoholics Anonymous should be strongly encouraged. Other medical and emotional problems that may interfere with a comfortable sobriety and a satisfying life without drinking should be identified and addressed whenever possible.

There is somewhat less agreement as to where treatment should take place and whether members of different professions should be treated with each other or in separate facilities. It is true that such specialized facilities have long existed for alcoholic priests, but there is no evidence that their treatment outcome was any better or worse in those settings than in places where persons from a variety of backgrounds are treated. Fichter compares segregated treatment with "mixed" facilities and finds fewer relapses (32% versus 40%) in special settings (2). Since all of the other settings are combined and we can say little about their quality, his study still does not provide a conclusive answer. Professionals are easy to treat along with others when they are not regarded as special and are allowed to assume the patient role. This does require an experienced staff capable of individualizing treatment (something they should be doing for every patient, not just the professional) and not likely to be overimpressed with any potentially "special" patient's occupation, power, or wealth and not distracted by how interested in the case the media may happen to be.

As staff turnover occurs, the quality of treatment at facilities changes. Many, however, have been treating alcoholic professionals of both sexes for many years with minimum fanfare and excellent results. These include Hazelden in Center City, Minnesota; Smithers Center at St. Luke's-Roosevelt Hospital in Manhattan; Chit Chat Farms in Wernersville, Pennsylvania; and Willingway in Statesboro, Georgia. Professionals like many affluent and powerful people have often been offered luxurious physical surroundings rather than evidence of good outcome, but, in general, good treatment for alcoholism does not mean expensive treatment—and often the reverse is true.

The sick physician, psychologist, or nurse must not be allowed to self-diagnose and to self-prescribe. If offered this opportunity, he or she will want to define the problem as symptomatic of something else, usually a problem or situation that cannot be changed. When it is obvious that something must be done, both the magnitude of the problem and the time and effort required to solve it will be minimized. Frequently, there will be an attempt to embroil the would-be helper in the reason why the illness exists rather than in what must be done about it. Alcoholics who can get someone else busy explaining why they drink or believing that insight alone will make things right are often able to get tacit approval to go right on drinking or taking prescription drugs, though for a time the amount will appear to decrease or the continued use may be concealed. Oftentimes residential treatment will be required and it may well have to be presented on an "or else" basis.

To force a person into treatment, insisting on cooperation with that treatment or threatening the loss of the right to practice, is to take on an enormous responsibility. If the treatment is wrong, it will not work. The old medical caveat of "above all, do no harm" must apply. Due process must not be forgotten simply because an alcoholic patient happens to be a physician or a priest. The treatment must fit the situation and the patient must not be allowed to choose ineffective treatment or to substitute process for outcome, with the excuse that he or she is seeing a therapist. By the same token, since there are many good treatment settings, the physician or attorney should be offered a choice as to which among several acceptable ones will be used. No single facility will be correct for all alcoholics in a profession.

PROGRAM CONSIDERATIONS

The design of each outreach program will of course depend on its setting as well as on local laws, politics, and the personalities involved, but it is possible to list what must be common considerations if a variety of different approaches are to work.

1. *Rapid response when needed.* A person attempting to care for another while obviously intoxicated or otherwise incapable of good judgment should be stopped at once. Other staff need to know how to sound the alert and that they really will be backed if they do.

2. *Prompt disposition.* Since reputation and livelihood are at stake, the person who has been stopped from practice deserves and needs a fast hearing. This provides some counterbalance for possibly too quick or arbitrary action.

3. *Protection of individual rights.* There should be as little invasion of privacy, gossip, and coercion as possible within the bounds of effective safeguards for the impaired person and the others affected.

4. *Suitable treatment.* Not only should the impaired person be given a choice of treatment programs or facilities of demonstrated effectiveness, but the nature of the problem must be correctly identified and the treatment appropriate.

5. *Rapid return to work.* Planning for aftercare as well as the initial treatment plan must be individualized and realistic. Some alcoholic professionals never have to leave home or stop practice. Others will require extended residential treatment. Ar-

bitrary insistence on periods of time away from practice is to be avoided.

6. *Realistic monitoring.*   Probably half of the alcoholic professionals who accept and cooperate with appropriate initial treatment will experience no further difficulty with drinking; the others will experience a relapse at some time. This is not a cause for alarm or discouragement, but there must be a plan for detection, firm and rapid intervention, and retreatment. A person is designated to monitor the patient's status and to move rapidly in case of trouble. The monitor should not be the person's therapist, since there would be an inevitable loyalty conflict should a return to drinking occur.

7. *Follow-up treatment plan.*   Most alcoholic patients do best if contact with a therapist or treatment team continues for two years. Interestingly, the duration seems to be more important than the type of treatment selected. A well-thought-out treatment plan that includes both patient and family will increase treatment success. If there are to be any reports made by the treatment team to family members, monitors, or disciplinary boards, the ground rules should be spelled out in advance to avoid misunderstandings in case of trouble.

8. *Reentry support.*   In addition to continued treatment and monitoring as noted above, contact should be arranged with appropriate self-help and support groups such as A.A., Narcotics Anonymous (N.A.), and Recovery Inc. These are available in almost infinite variety, even in many smaller communities. It is also helpful if other colleagues can arrange some form of welcome back from treatment. Too often both friends and patient feel awkward with one another and are reluctant to talk about what has happened. Shyness may lead to mutual avoidance, and then to distancing and isolation. Wonderful though a self-help group may be, it may still be experienced in part as an acceptance only by fellow outcasts, while the real world of former friends is now seen as hostile and unavailable. One woman said, "They were polite enough, but they were too uncomfortable to talk about it so they talked about the weather and gave me hooded looks when they thought I wasn't looking."

9. *Adequate publicity.*   A service is widely used only when its availability is known and its credibility established. Since questions and referrals may come from many directions, information

must reach members of the profession, family members, patients, and the concerned public. Information should be very specific and very clear to minimize anxiety about confidentiality and about who will answer the telephone, what questions will be asked, and who can call and when. This same information must be given repeatedly since it may be rejected many times by those who need it before the circumstances finally are right for it to be heard and used.

INSURANCE

A check on group health insurance policies sold under the sponsorship of a variety of alumni, national, or state professional organizations reveals that treatment for alcoholism and addiction is frequently excluded from coverage. One can only speculate as to why the professions have permitted this. Probably the root of it is the belief that alcoholism will spare us and our families, that it will remain someone else's illness. No one plans or expects to be alcoholic. A bout of pneumonia seems very possible, dental caries almost a certainty, but not alcoholism. As for others, there may perhaps be an unwillingness to pay for treatment for what appears to be a self-inflicted illness.

While speculating, it is worthwhile to check the coverage provided in our own policies. If we, our colleagues, or family members develop an alcohol problem or drug problem, will insurance provide a reasonable amount of treatment? In an appropriate specialized facility or only in an acute care or psychiatric hospital? Will any outpatient care be included? Will the family be covered?

Obviously an important consideration in the planning of treatment is confronting the financial realities of the situation. It is terribly frustrating to have a colleague or family member admit to a long-denied problem, agree to treatment, and then discover that the insurance coverage is too little or for the wrong type of facility. An alcoholic may well need treatment most when financial resources are low and there will be no income for a time. It is also frustrating when an alcoholic colleague is forced to accept the additional stigma of an inaccurate psychiatric label in order to gain hospital admission. The fact that after the initial period of physical detoxification (which often is not even necessary) less expensive and frequently better care is available in other residential but nonhospital facilities makes this particularly unfortunate.

Many insurance companies claim that the necessary comprehensive coverage is not available or that it can be had only at greatly increased premiums. This simply is not true, but one needs to be persistent and perhaps may need to change carriers.

THE FAMILY

While planning for the alcoholic, family members must not be overlooked. They are usually the first to be aware of the drinking problem as well as to be deeply affected by it. They are unlikely to know what help is available and what steps to take. Love and loyalty blend with the anxiety that they themselves are causing the problem. Fear and ignorance leave them immobilized. While some groups have mailed information to family members about hotlines and advocacy groups, others have sent materials only to the professionals themselves. Unfortunately, as alcoholism progresses, all those involved tend to withdraw from outside activities and become less likely to belong to professional societies. Many doctors and their spouses never join medical societies and auxiliaries in the first place. Ways must be found to reach those who have simply stopped paying dues as well as those who may have lost licenses and been written off in the days when alcoholism and its treatment were less well understood.

Consider too the dilemma of the professional whose spouse is the drinker. To live with an actively drinking alcoholic is an exercise in unpredictability, bewilderment, and uncertainty. As is any other husband or wife, the doctor, nurse, or attorney may be unsure whether this is really alcoholism or an underlying emotional problem of some sort, perhaps even a problem rooted in the marriage itself. In spite of all the knowledge from a graduate education, this distress in one's own family often simply does not respond to one's efforts to heal. Shame and concealment may be as great as for any other family, sometimes even greater, since often the nurse or physician foolishly starts to medicate the drinking spouse, knows it to be wrong, and then is even more embarrassed at the idea that others will know.

Meantime the professional's own career suffers as worries increase about whether or not children are being cared for, automobile accidents are occurring, or burning cigarettes are dropped on the furniture. One surgeon described his situation as one in which he is always on call, constantly needing to be near a telephone, afraid not to go home to check on things, and equally afraid of what he would find when he did.

While perhaps the "special" treatment required by the alcoholic professional is simply not to be treated as "special," this does not mean, alcoholic or not, that they can pretend to be exactly like others. Insofar as judges, doctors, nurses, and priests still command the respect of the public and are seen by them as role models, we must accept that they face higher expectations than those made of others. They are no less human or vulnerable than anyone else, and yet professionals do have unique skills, resources, and abilities to plan for themselves and help their colleagues. Alcoholism is not a disease that anyone plans to get, and one certainly does not expect it to occur in one's own family or close professional community, but it does happen to professionals as well as to others. The task then is to be ready. Thoughtful planning takes time and should not be delayed until there is a crisis.

DENIAL AND THE ACCEPTANCE OF TREATMENT

While some alcoholic and drug-dependent people readily admit to a problem when challenged, rather easily agree to accept treatment, and may even seem relieved that things have come to a head, most will do no such thing. Self-delusion and denial to self and others are integral parts of the problem. Anger, underestimation of the problem, excuses, defensiveness, and counterattack can be expected. Intervention and confrontation must be carefully planned, and those who intercede should be familiar with the techniques for making these approaches (3).

Crucial to a successful result will be careful documentation of those observations that have caused concern, firmness without anger or accusation, and a clear agreement on what the intervention is to accomplish. If the goal is to gain an agreement to enter treatment, insistence on a signed confession is not necessary. It is also important that no threats be made unless there is full ability and willingness to carry them out. When persuasion does not work, the "or else" may well be needed.

ADVOCACY VERSUS COERCIVE METHODS

Some professional groups function entirely in a noncoercive, persuasive, and advocacy role, yet can be effective in getting the reluctant into treatment. They receive self-referrals as well as take action on cases referred by others, but they keep only minimal records, make no reports, and will not undertake to force any colleague to do anything. Using this approach are Lawyers Concerned for Lawyers (LCL), Dentists Concerned for Dentists (DCD), and Physicians Serving Physicians (PSP), all in Minnesota. (See Appendix C for these and similar groups.)

The noncoercive groups usually work as follows. A group of concerned professionals forms, initially almost exclusively composed of those having personal experience with alcoholism or addiction. (Others later join, so that to be known as a group member does not automatically label anyone. These members often help sort out psychiatric problems that may be beyond the capacity of the early membership.) The group is usually organized after individuals learn with some dismay that formal disciplinary procedures come into play only after impairment is quite advanced, and even then they move sluggishly, reach only a small number of those needing help, and are used quite reluctantly, if at all, by colleagues.

Impatient and dissatisfied with the existing system, they resolve to create a parallel system that can respond earlier in the course of the illness as well as more promptly. They recognize that, without strict confidentiality, people are quite unlikely to call for help or to refer a peer. They become aware that, if they were to do anything to harm a colleague's reputation or to meddle very deeply in anyone's private life, then due process, the right to privacy, and the risk of litigation would become major considerations. They resolve not to reveal what they learn or to use any power other than that of persuasion and example. Anyone can call and request their help for self or for someone else. Although the group will learn enough about the caller to be sure the call is not simply an attempt to harass, they will agree not to tell the alcoholic who has blown the whistle. Since in no way will the group harm the alcoholic, there are few worries about the right to know and face an "accuser."

The group makes its presence known and slowly referrals do come. Anonymous calls of the "I have this friend" variety are common, so that providing information about professional policy and procedures or about treatment resources becomes an additional function. Colleagues already in trouble with licensing boards or hospital privileges call wanting help with reentry problems or hoping that the group will advocate in their behalf, usually by attesting to the duration or quality of their recovery.

There are almost immediate misunderstandings from a variety of outsiders about what the group is trying to do. In spite of repeated statements that only minimal records are kept, there are demands for data on "results of this treatment" and a great deal of anxiety expressed over the idea that the group knows of people dangerous to the public yet fails to report them. Pressure to work more closely with enforcement agencies builds.

With experience, group members become aware that skill as an intervenor does not automatically follow from simply "having been there." The Minnesota groups sought training for their members at the Johnson Institute, a nonprofit Minneapolis organization that has pioneered in intervention training for families, therapists, and managers. (This organization can also provide films and literature as well as send trainers to other states since it is obviously not feasible for large groups to travel to Minnesota.)

With better preparation, intervention results improve. Teams of group members call on their troubled colleagues and persuade many of them into treatment. LCL, DCD, and PSP limit their role to intervention and referral. Although they share a full-time employee who is a trained counselor, they do not attempt to provide treatment themselves and are careful to avoid the appearance of a conflict of interest.

When admission for treatment occurs, or when it is clear that even repeated contacts are unlikely to be effective, the case is closed and records destroyed. Statistics are limited to the number and general type of problems encountered, whether or not contact is made, and a brief note on outcome. One can say about LCL, for instance, that since its beginning in 1976 its membership grew from 7 to 75 in 18 months and that, during that period, LCL was instrumental in getting over 70 alcoholic judges and lawyers into some form of treatment (4).

Increased demand for service usually leads to the recognition that there is simply too much work and out-of-pocket expense involved for volunteers to handle. Expenses and staff time require some manner of funding. In Minnesota, the bar association and state medical and dental societies have contributed to a shared office on a "no-strings-attached" basis. (These are, of course, the relatively large and wealthy professional groups. It remains to be seen whether or not ANA or NASW state chapters can or will follow suit.)

THE COERCIVE APPROACH

Every licensed profession has some sort of state-level agency charged with granting or revoking licenses. Usually housed within either a department of health or of education, it receives complaints both from the public and from fellow professionals. When alerted that a problem exists, it sends out investigators to look into the matter. If the investigators are able to establish the accuracy of the complaint, the professional will be notified, advised of his or her rights, and asked to appear with counsel for a hearing. Many states have far too few investigators to look into more than the most serious cases and many are seriously backlogged. The early alcoholic—who may never have had an arrest, may never have hurt a patient, may never have done anything more clear-cut than overdrink at times or miss an occasional obligation—can easily escape discipline. With no documented episode of harm to patient or client, no formal complaint, and no measured blood alcohol concentration recorded, how is the state to prove that this person is drinking more than anyone else? Family, patients, office nurse, or secretary may have seen a great deal more, yet be understandably reluctant to act.

It is much easier to investigate doctors, nurses, and pharmacists for suspected diversion of prescription drugs than to measure the extent of their alcohol problems. Records of controlled drugs are available; records of alcohol sales to individuals are not kept and would prove little if they were. Even being drunk on many occasions does not necessarily prove alcoholism, while one single event can show that the law concerning narcotics has been broken. A California lawyers' group offers 20 questions for their alcoholic colleagues to use in addition to other self-tests for alcoholism.

(See Appendix D.) Few of these questions could be answered with certainty by anyone but the attorney concerned or someone very close to that person and likely to be very loyal. In any event, state boards cannot act without evidence, and convincing evidence of early and even middle-stage alcoholism sufficient for their purposes may be hard to obtain.

STATE PROFESSIONAL ORGANIZATIONS

The special committees of professional organizations concerned with ethics, professional standards, or impairment stand separate from most of the advocacy groups and from state government. These committees receive complaints from the public on everything from minor public relations problems and disputes over billings to serious charges of professional misconduct. Most have power only to threaten to report to the board or to expel a member from the organization itself. The effect on an individual of such an expulsion may be serious or trivial. Many professionals never join these organizations, although some hospitals, for instance, have required their medical staff to be "eligible for membership" in a local medical society, even though they are not forced to be members as a condition of the right to admit patients. For a surgeon who depends on hospital privileges in order to work, this is obviously important. For a psychiatrist in private practice, it may be at best a minor annoyance.

These committees vary widely in what they attempt to do and how they go about it. Some are very active and very inventive; others are largely ineffectual. Many of them borrow the techniques of the noncoercive groups, call on their troubled colleagues, and attempt to persuade them into treatment, but if gentleness and reason fail, they are likely to threaten to report to the board and often will do so. If an actively dangerous person cannot or will not cooperate, they are free to act at once by turning that person in. What actually occurs in a given state or given profession will vary with the organization, its policies, the local laws, and, above all, with local politics and personalities. None have achieved perfection.

A recent development has been the hiring of staff by state societies to work with troubled professionals. In New Jersey in 1982, David I. Canavan, M.D., was selected to work full time for the New Jersey Medical Association as director of their impaired physician program. Initially predicting that he would work with about 40 physicians in his first year, he found himself involved with over 70 in his first eight months on the job and frequently with their families as well (5). He too is careful not to become involved in actual treatment. His role includes intervention, referral, and monitoring plus a great deal of time devoted to the education of colleagues and hospital administrators. Other states and organizations have begun to follow suit.

Since these committees and staff people can do an effective job, the need for the noncoercive groups to continue as well is constantly questioned. If they have no actual power, create an additional expense, and are destined to fail most of the time, why should they continue to exist at all? How can they fail to report people who may be in danger or endangering others?

Granted that the nature of these groups precludes defending them by citing outcome statistics, it should nevertheless be pointed out that anyone reporting a person to such a group remains free to report the information at the same time or at a later date to one of the more coercive agencies. These actions are not mutually exclusive and the person placing the complaint is usually so informed. Since people are notoriously reluctant to "tattle" on one another, particularly since they may be afraid of being identified as the tale-bearer, they tend to procrastinate until undesirable situations are quite advanced. People sincerely question their own motives, agonize over the possibility that they are unduly suspicious, and are wary that to report a friend may do more harm than good. Many, sometimes with good reason, see boards and committees as ineffective, slow, and sometimes actually destructive rather than helpful. If offered another choice, someone to call who may fail to help but will at least do no harm, many hesitant witnesses will report much sooner than they ordinarily might.

A DESIRABLE SEQUENCE OF STEPS

There is room for more than one approach to getting a colleague into treatment. Actions logically should progress from those easily taken on an informal basis by friends and family to those taken by the extended family of peers and colleagues with whom one works. At any point the noncoercive group, if available, can be asked to assist. If that does not work, a hospital or other employee assistance program or committee at the workplace may sometimes be able to effect the desired result (6,7). If it in turn cannot, then a state society's committee may succeed. If all else fails, the final step of reporting to a state disciplinary board can be taken.

The one action most certain to be wrong is to do nothing—to protect and nurture until, as an alcoholic nun put it, "We were actually loved to death."

PREVENTION

At each AMA Impaired Physicians Conference there has been increasing interest not just in secondary prevention (early discovery and intervention to alter the course of an already existing illness) but primary prevention as well. Suggestions are also made for identifying high-risk people and perhaps actually barring them from professional training in the first place (8), but the cost of that approach is rapidly seen to be too high for whatever benefit it might offer.

Another suggestion asks that better information be made available earlier in the course of professional training that might help all concerned. Some 90 percent of all attorneys and physicians are drinkers (9), and most of the students who are going to drink are already doing so before they begin their postgraduate education (10,11). Knowledge is desirable in its own right, and certainly students need to know a great deal more than they presently do about alcoholism in their patients, their communities, their colleagues, and themselves. They need to know what to do about it. Whether they can use that knowledge to avoid alcohol problems in their own lives is another matter, one that has yet to be studied.

Even more tempting is the hope that, if students are taught about the hazards and stresses of their own professions, they will develop healthier life-styles that will, in turn, decrease the likelihood of overworking, neglect of marriages and friendships, midlife depression, and the like. If overdrinking is seen as a response to these other problems and if overdrinking is seen as the necessary precursor of alcoholism, it is suggested that measures that promote emotional well-being may succeed.

We already know of ways to decrease some of the occupational stress that so often makes self-medication with drugs and alcohol so attractive. For those professionals who have to work different shifts, for instance, we might use already available knowledge on sleep disturbance, emotional upset, and their relationship to disrupted circadian rhythms to change the timing and sequence of alterations in work schedules. For nurses and house officers in particular, this simple maneuver would go far to help with a long-standing problem (12). But would it prevent anyone at all from becoming alcoholic?

Probably the etiology of alcoholism is too complex for any simple maneuvers to prevent it altogether, but better teaching and a more human environment for students are certainly needed, for many other reasons as well. The influence of our total upbringing and our surrounding society, of which the professional school environment and the influence of peers are only a part, probably will outweigh, but not render futile or invalid, much that we attempt to do for one another.

There are many ways to make a difference. Information alone will not prevent or cure alcoholism, but it needs to be made available. To make sound education on alcoholism a mandatory part of professional training in many fields would make excellent sense, since it is too common a problem for clients, patients, students, and peers to allow the current neglect to be justified.

Brown University's president, Howard R. Swearer, Ph.D., recently took a simple but important step. He has set a policy that whenever a campus social event involves drinking alcohol, an attractive nonalcoholic beverage must also be available. This not only provides a choice for problem drinkers but makes life easier for diabetics, hypertensives, epileptics, the calorie conscious, the recent hepatitis patient, and all the others who for a variety of reasons either would prefer not to or should not drink. The wine and cheese party limited entirely to wine and cheese is actually more thoughtless than stylish.

Although it might prove surprisingly difficult to reach a consensus on so simple a policy, it might be well, particularly for those who give direct care to others and must make important decisions in their behalf, to discourage as strongly as possible any drinking immediately before seeing patients or clients. Does it really lend anything beneficial to a treatment situation when the professional smells of alcohol? The aroma of one drink is much the same as that of half a dozen, and it is so important to have the confidence of a client, a patient, or a friend. This would mean taking a hard look at specific situations such as lunchtime drinking and whether or not that is seen as an issue of importance. If it is, to whom is it important and why?

In our concern for students and other young people we are struck repeatedly with the importance of peer pressure and the influence of role models in shaping the behavior of our young colleagues. If initially the important role models are our parents, later they are replaced by mentors, faculty and practitioners, supervisors, and consultants whom we observe, admire, and emulate. What they do we are likely to do. A most telling part of professional training is this informal apprenticeship that may occur entirely outside of the classroom and that depends largely on what we learn about each others' lives in myriad ways. Perhaps a necessary first step for someone who really wants to help is to ask a simple question: Do I really want this young man or young woman to drink exactly the way I do?

REFERENCES

1. M. D. Vincent, "Physicians after 65," *Canadian Medical Association Journal 120*: 1979, pp. 998–99.

2. J. H. Fichter, "Ardent Spirits Subdued," in: *The Occupational Connection, Proceedings of the 15th Annual Eagleville Conference*, Eagleville, Pa.: May 1982, pp. 222–29.

3. V. E. Johnson, *I'll Quit Tomorrow: A Breakthrough Treatment for Alcoholism* (revised edition), New York: Harper and Row, 1980.

4. LCL, Lawyers Concerned for Lawyers, Minneapolis, 1978.

5. D. Canavan, Personal Communication, 1983.

6. G. Jackson, "An Employee Alcoholism Program for Nurses and Social Workers," *Labor-Management Alcoholism Journal 9*: November–December 1979, pp. 115–22.

7. L. Bissell and K. Lambrecht, "The Alcoholic Hospital Employee," *Nursing Outlook 21*: November 1973, pp. 708–11.

8. S. C. Scheiber and B. B. Doyle, "Recommendations," in: *The Impaired Physician*, New York: Plenum Press, 1983.

9. G. Wyshak et al., "Profile of the Health-Promoting Behaviors of Physicians and Lawyers," *New England Journal of Medicine 303*: July 10, 1980, pp. 104–7.

10. M. Lipp et al., "Medical Student Use of Marijuana, Alcohol and Cigarettes: A Study of Four Schools," *International Journal of the Addictions 7*: 1972, pp. 141–52.

11. H. Wechsler and M. Rohman, "Future Leaders' Views on Alcohol Use and Misuse," *Journal of Studies on Alcohol 43*: 1982, pp. 1084–96.

12. M. C. Moore-Ede et al., "Circadian Timekeeping in Health and Disease: Part 2. Clinical Implications of Circadian Rhythmicity," *New England Journal of Medicine 309*: September 1, 1983, pp. 530–36.

Appendixes

Appendix A. Abridged Items in Initial Interview and Reinterview[a]

Item Description	Initial Interview	Reinterview
Profession	2.1	2.1, 6.4
Follow-up respondent—subject or informant		6.1, 6.2
Interview date	*	*
Interviewer	*	*
Residence	*	*
Sex	2.1	
Age	2.1, 6.4	
Birthplace	*	
Religion now and parents' religions	*	
Parents' occupations	*	
Marital status	*	*
Times married	*	
Children—number and age	*	
Living arrangement	*	
Military service and type of discharge	*	
Current annual gross earned income	*	
Other income	*	
Total family income	*	
Age when held most prestigious job before stopped drinking; when this job began and ended	*	
Total time of unemployment because of drinking	*	
Age when graduated college or prenursing school	*	
Honors or Phi Beta Kappa in college	*	

[a]The asterisk (*) indicates that the item appears in the interview. A table number is indicated when an item appears in a table within the book. In the initial interview, a few items were not asked of all professions; several others were not posed in as much detail to all professions. In the reinterview, the same items were asked of all professions studied.

193

Item Description	Initial Interview	Reinterview
Age when professional degree or license received, and other educational details	*	
Further specialty training		*
Class standing in professional school	3.3	
Occupational details	*	
Principal activity now—work status	*	*
Time spent with alcoholic patients/ clients	*	*
Time otherwise professionally concerned with alcoholism	*	*
Age at first occurrence of drinking-related experiences	3.1, 3.2	
Relation of person who first expressed concern about drinking	*	
Experiences related to alcoholism	4.3	
Legal sanctions	4.1	*
Professional sanctions	4.1, 4.4	*
Other mood-changing drug use—type of drug, prescribed, addiction, how taken	3.4, 6.4	6.3
Mood-changing drugs taken now—reason and other details	*	6.3
Other mood-changing drug use before first interview		*
Time sequence of use and abuse of alcohol, nonnarcotic drugs, "hard" narcotics, and codeine	*	6.3
Time sequence of use and abuse of alcohol, nonnarcotic drugs, "hard" narcotics, and codeine before first interview		*
Smoking—change in frequency and method		3.5
Inpatient admissions for alcoholism, alcohol-related illness, or other drug abuse—number, length of stay, age	4.2	*
Outpatient treatment, before A.A., for alcoholism—by psychiatrist,		

Item Description	Initial Interview	Reinterview
other physician, other professional, and nonprofessional	*	
Told was not an alcoholic	*	
Hospitalization for condition *not* related to alcoholism or other drug abuse—number, length of stay, age:		
During five years, before A.A. sobriety	*	
After A.A. sobriety	*	*
Outpatient psychiatric and other professional treatment after A.A. sobriety	*	*
Serious overdose—number, age, drugs, and other details	*	*
Suicide attempts—number, age, method, and other details	*	*
Where and age when first heard of A.A.	*	
Circumstances of and age at first A.A. contact	*	
Age when first attended A.A. meeting	3.1, 3.2	
Age at first occurrence for other A.A. participation	*	
Age when had last drink	3.1, 3.2, 6.4	
A.A. attendance now	5.2	*
Member of which types of A.A. groups	*	*
Participation in A.A. activities— during and before last six months	*	*
Socializing with A.A. members outside of A.A. meetings	*	*
To whom A.A. membership is known	*	*
Reasons given for declining drinking in social situations	*	*
Serve alcoholic beverages at home	5.3	*
Would, if could, drink safely	5.3, 6.4	*
Slips since first attended A.A. meetings over five-week period	6.4	

Item Description	Initial Interview	Reinterview
Immediate family member alcoholic, in A.A., in Al-Anon—father, mother, spouse, siblings, children	6.4	*
Alcoholism primarily physical/biochemical or mental/emotional/psychological	*	6.4
Alcoholism inherited	*	*
Believe alcoholic can ever return safely to normal drinking	5.3, 6.4	*
Expectations regarding A.A. emphasis on religion	*	5.1
Expectations regarding socioeconomic level of A.A. members	*	5.1
Number known, in same profession, reasonably certain to have serious drinking problem (excluding sober A.A. members)	*	*
Number of days drinking in each of five years since first interview		6.1, 6.3, 6.4
Quality of and reason for drinking since first interview		*

Appendix B. The Twelve Suggested Steps of Alcoholics Anonymous[a]

1. We admitted we were powerless over alcohol—that our lives had become unmanageable.

2. Came to believe that a Power greater than ourselves could restore us to sanity.

3. Made a decision to turn our will and our lives over to the care of God, *as we understood Him.*

4. Made a searching and fearless moral inventory of ourselves.

5. Admitted to God, to ourselves and to another human being the exact nature of our wrongs.

6. Were entirely ready to have God remove all these defects of character.

7. Humbly asked Him to remove our shortcomings.

8. Made a list of all persons we had harmed, and became willing to make amends to them all.

9. Made direct amends to such people wherever possible, except when to do so would injure them or others.

10. Continued to take personal inventory, and when we were wrong promptly admitted it.

11. Sought through prayer and meditation to improve our conscious contact with God *as we understood Him,* praying only for knowledge of His will for us and the power to carry that out.

12. Having had a spiritual awakening as the result of these steps, we tried to carry this message to alcoholics, and to practice these principles in all our affairs.

Alcoholics Anonymous is a fellowship of men and women who share their experience, strength and hope with each other that they may solve their common problem and help others to recover from alcoholism.

The only requirement for membership is a desire to stop drinking. There are no dues or fees for A.A. membership; we are self-supporting

---

[a]Excerpts used with permission of the General Service Office of Alcoholics Anonymous.

through our own contributions. A.A. is not allied with any sect, denomination, politics, organization or institution; does not wish to engage in any controversy, neither endorses nor opposes any causes. Our primary purpose is to stay sober and help other alcoholics to achieve sobriety.

Appendix C. Professional Groups and Organizations Dealing with Alcoholism and Drug Dependency

A. Limited to alcoholic or chemically dependent people.

1. *Attorneys*

   International Lawyers in A.A. (ILAA)
   111 Pearl Street, Room 202
   Hartford, Connecticut 06103
   (203) 527-1854

   English Alcoholic Group for Lawyers (EAGL)
   A. Robinson, M.A., Co-Ordinator
   Morrab Villa, PENZANCE
   Cornwall TR18 4DQ, U.K.
   0736.68369

   or

   English Alcoholic Group for Lawyers (EAGL)
   John Eccles
   1 Stoneham House
   13 Queens Road
   Richmond, Surrey TW10 6JW
   01.940.9163

2. *Clergy* (Anglican)

   Recovered Alcoholic Clergy Assn. (RACA)
   647 Dundee Avenue
   Barrington, Illinois 60010
   (312) 381-2323

3. *Psychologists*

   Psychologists Helping Psychologists
   Jane Skorina, Ph.D.
   23439 Michigan Street
   Dearborn, Michigan 48124
   (313) 565-3821

B. Limited to those who have had a personal (rather than professional) experience with alcoholism or other chemical dependency. Includes Al-Anon members.

  1. *Physicians, dentists, and other doctoral-level, health-care professionals*

     International Doctors in A.A.
     1950 Volney Road
     Youngstown, Ohio 44511
     (216) 782-6216

  2. *Nurses*—See NNSA (E-2, below)

  3. *Social Workers*

     Social Workers Helping Social Workers
     Contact:
     John F. Fitzgerald, M.S.W., Ph.D.
     Route #63
     Goshen, Connecticut 06756
     (203) 491-2490 or (203) 566-2696

C. Composed largely of persons having had personal experience with alcoholism or chemical dependency but members include others.

  1. *Attorneys*

     Lawyers Concerned for Lawyers
     610 Chamber of Commerce Bldg.
     15 5th Street South
     Minneapolis, Minnesota 55402
     (612) 339-1230

  2. *Anthropologists*

     Anthropologists Concerned for Anthropologists
     c/o James M. Schaefer, Ph.D.
     Office of Alcohol and Other Drug Abuse Programming
     Room 360
     2610 University Avenue
     St. Paul, Minnesota 55114

3. *Clergy (Catholic)*

National Clergy Council on Alcoholism and Related Drug
    Problems
3112 7th Street N.E.
Washington, D.C. 20017
(202) 832-3811

4. *Nuns (Catholic)*

ICAP
2510 N. Drake
Chicago, Illinois 60647
(312) 342-1413

5. *Dentists*

Dentists Concerned for Dentists
610 Chamber of Commerce Bldg.
15 5th Street South
Minneapolis, Minnesota 55402
(612) 339-1068

6. *Physicians*

Physicians Serving Physicians
610 Chamber of Commerce Bldg.
15 5th Street South
Minneapolis, Minnesota 55402
(612) 339-0711

British Doctor's Group
c/o The Medical Council on Alcoholism
3 Grosvenor Crescent, London SWIX, U.K.
01-235-4182
(*Correspondence can be marked "Please forward unopened" if
desired.*)

7. *Gay/lesbian (multidisciplinary)*

National Association of Gay Alcoholism Professionals
Dana Finnigan, Ph.D.
204 W. 20th Street
New York, New York 10011
(212) 807-0634

The organizations listed above (sections A, B, and C) are primarily advocacy and support groups and will not attempt to coerce, discipline, or police those who seek their help. There are many state-level groups and committees. Some are limited to offering help, keep no records, make no reports to other agencies, and avoid any attempt to manage or monitor. Others are frankly disciplinary and operate more as extensions of licensing boards. Still others have combined functions. All 50 state medical societies now have impaired physician committees.

D. State associations and professional organizations *not* primarily composed of recovered individuals.

1. *Catholic Nuns (includes nursing orders)*

   Sister Maurice Doody
   Office of New Directions
   2341 University Avenue
   Bronx, New York 10468
   (212) 365-5730

2. *Dentists*

   Council on Dental Practice
   American Dental Association
   211 East Chicago Avenue
   Chicago, Illinois 60611
   (800) 621-8099
     Contact: H. Kendal Beachman, Secretary
        or

   Dr. John C. Clarno
   Special Consultant
   ADA Alcohol/Drug Program
   Parkside Medical
   1580 N. Northwest Highway
   Park Ridge, Illinois 60068
   (312) 696-8200

3. *Pharmacists*

   Richard P. Penna, Pharm.D.
   American Pharmaceutical Assn.
   2215 Constitution Avenue, N.W.
   Washington, D.C. 20037
   (202) 628-4410

4. *Physicians*

Health and Human Behavior Program
AMA
535 North Dearborn Street
Chicago, Illinois 60610
(312) 751-6000
(Maintains list of impaired physician committees.)

George Esselman, D.O.
Texas College of Osteopathic Medicine
Camp Bowie at Montgomery Street
Ft. Worth, Texas 76107
(817) 735-2561
(Has information about state committees within osteopathic medicine.)

5. *Nurses*

Several states, including Ohio and Maryland, now have impaired
nurse committees and will share information through their state
nursing associations.

E. Professional organizations that focus on alcoholism and chemical
   dependence whose memberships are limited to specific disciplines
   and who have available information on specific committees within
   their ranks for helping impaired colleagues.

1. *Clergy* (*interfaith*)

North Conway Institute
14 Beacon Street
Boston, Massachusetts 02108

2. *Nurses*

Drug and Alcohol Nursing Assn., Inc. (DANA)
Box 371
College Park, Maryland 20740

National Nurses Society on Addictions (NNSA)
2506 Gross Point Road
Evanston, Illinois 60201

One professional working in Kansas is assembling a directory of A.A. and other support groups for nurses and is already able to direct callers to many groups and individuals:

> Pat Green, R.N.
> 1020 Sunset Drive
> Lawrence, Kansas 66044
> (913) 842-3893

3. *Physicians*

> American Medical Society on Alcoholism
> 12 West 21 Street
> New York, New York 10010
> (212) 206-6770

There are over 40 local groups for medical professionals which are similar to, but independent of, IDAA. Many other groups for special populations exist, such as:

> JACS Foundation
> c/o New York Board of Rabbis
> 10 East 73rd Street
> New York, New York 10021
> (212) 737-6261

which provides networking and support services to Jewish alcoholics and has a large number of professionals in its membership.

General

Many of these groups are known to the General Service Office of Alcoholics Anonymous, Box 459, Grand Central Station, New York, New York 10163, and, while not listed in official A.A. directories, are on file. Although interested in the more broad promotion of physical and mental well-being rather than in alcoholism per se and primarily for health-care professionals, additional information and materials can be obtained from:

> Center for Professional Well-Being
> 5102 Chapel Hill Blvd.
> Durham, North Carolina 27707
> (919) 489-9167

In 1983 an association of employee assistance programs that provides services to hospitals was formed. It plans to share information, develop standards, and provide general support. Contact through:

> Association of Labor-Management Administrators and
>   Consultants on Alcoholism (ALMACA)
> 1800 North Kent Street
> Suite 907
> Arlington, Virginia 22209
> (703) 522-6272

The authors would appreciate being made aware of similar groups.

Appendix D.   20 Questions Developed by California Lawyers for Their Colleagues

Judge Leon Emerson's California committee for assisting impaired attorneys has made 20 questions specifically applicable to the conduct of lawyers. (Comparable sets of questions might be designed for other professions.)

To the attorney: Answering "yes" to three or more of the following questions indicates a strong possibility of alcoholism.

1. Have you failed to show up at the office because of a hangover, the jitters, or shakes?
2. Failed to appear in court for the same reason?
3. Neglected to process mail promptly?
4. Neglected to pay state bar dues on time?
5. Frequently failed to keep appointments?
6. Showed up in court or at depositions under the influence?
7. Are you drinking in the office during office hours?
8. Have you used—misused—commingled or borrowed clients' trust funds?
9. Have you failed to accept or answer telephone calls because you didn't feel good?
10. Have you gotten other attorneys to make court appearances on your behalf?
11. Are you avoiding the resolution of problems?
12. Are you regularly partaking of noontime cocktails?
13. Is your ability to perform diminished in the afternoon?
14. Are you frequently blaming your secretary for the things that go wrong?
15. Is your relationship with your clients, staff, and friends deteriorating?
16. Do you get drunk at bar association meetings and social gatherings?
17. Does your spouse complain you are drinking too much?
18. Are you missing deadlines for performance like allowing the Statute of Limitations to run out?
19. Are you losing control at social gatherings when professional decorum is called for?
20. Are these occurrences increasing in their frequency?

OTHER SIGNS are lying to cover up your drinking, justifying your right to drink, giving excuses to take a drink.

If you were to apply to your own drinking life the same evidentiary tests that you apply to a legal problem, you would find that there is no evidence on which to base the statement that "This time will be different." Only an alcoholic finds repugnant the idea of never taking another drink; only an alcoholic would feel that he couldn't live life without alcohol; only an alcoholic would think that this test is unfair and that anyone who drinks would have to answer the above questions affirmatively.

Index

Page numbers followed by *t* indicate tables.

209